10-20-73

**Rightly
Dividing
the Word**

Rightly Dividing the Word

DORAN MC CARTY

BROADMAN PRESS
Nashville, Tennessee

Library of Congress Catalog Card Number: 73–78217
Dewey Decimal Classification: 220.6
Printed in the United States of America

Preface

The Bible has become so much a part of my way of life that it is like breath to me. I assume its life-giving presence just as I assume that my lungs will breathe air. Perhaps, it is only the controversy aroused by those to my right and left which keeps bringing back to my consciousness the spiritual oxygen that I breathe—the Bible.

As is true with many, my parents gave me my first appreciation for the Bible. It is for this reason that I dedicate this book to them.

I am deeply grateful to my secretary, Mrs. Shirley Mynatt, who has worked so hard to prepare this manuscript from tapes and rough notes and prior to deadlines. I appreciate the helpfulness of my colleague Professor Kenneth Wolfe, especially for his guidance toward the illustrations found in chapter 12.

*This book is dedicated
to my parents,
Bartie Lee McCarty
and
Donta Marian Russell McCarty*

Prayer of Dedication

O God
    of majesty and love;
We seek to follow thee down the paths of life
Until at last we are with thee for eternity.

We recognize the Scriptures
    To be our guide to thee;
    To be the light which shines on our path to thee;
    To be the warning signs to keep us from straying
        from thee.
We know that the Scriptures
    Tell us of thy majesty;
    Point us to thy love;
    Warn us of thy judgment;
    Enlighten us of thy plan.
We hold the Scriptures to be holy as they have been
    Made sacred by the Spirit in his inspiring them;
    Made sacred by thy church in her choosing them;
    Made sacred by the saints by using them.
We go to the Scriptures because we
    Seek the love of God;
    Search the truth of God;
    Desire what is good for man;
    Covet what is right for ourselves.

We confess that the Scriptures speak to us about
>The faith we should have for the unknown;
>The love we should have for the unwanted;
>The hope we should have in the unseen.

Lord, O Lord,
Let the Scriptures speak to us!
Let us not be blinded by our prejudice;
Let the Scriptures speak to us again
>Out of the freshness of new experiences with thee;
Let the Scriptures speak to us again
>Out of the needs of our own souls;
Let the Scriptures speak to us again
>Out of the crises of a troubled world.

Lord, our Lord,
Thou art our God.
We thank thee
>That thou hast not kept silent but hast spoken
>through the prophets, Jesus Christ, and now
>through Scriptures.
We thank thee
>That thou hast not left us orphans but art present
>in thy Spirit through the Scriptures.
We thank thee
>For our salvation now and forever more;
>For Jesus Christ who made it possible; and
>For the Bible which made it known.

Contents

1

Rightly Dividing the Word

"Study to shew thyself approved unto God, a workman that needeth not to be ashamed, rightly dividing the word of truth" (2 Tim. 2:15).

Christianity has been struggling with the proper handling of the Bible. When the Revised Standard Version was translated, many attacked it with charges of heresy, atheism, and communism. There were instances where copies of the RSV were gathered up and burned. Recently, there have been attacks made on "Good News for Modern Man," a rendering of the New Testament into everyday English speech.

Denominations have faced breaches of fellowship and possible fractures over biblical interpretations. A great deal of time in recent sessions of the Southern Baptist Convention has been given to debating issues of biblical interpretation. The Missouri Synod Lutherans have recently undergone investigations for heresy which were centered in biblical interpretation.

Laymen in churches have become involved in the disputes about how to interpret the Bible. Some have accused their pastors of liberalism or fanaticism. Others have frantically sought clear-cut answers from the Bible about modern problems such as amnesty, abortion, and space exploration. Inasmuch as many secular books give precise answers to specific questions, many laymen are frustrated that their questions do not have precisely matching answers in the Bible. They are asking, "How *can* we rightly divide the Word of God?"

Many voices have attempted to answer this question. Some have said that the truth of the Bible is obvious and all you have to do is read it. Once you have read it, believe it literally the way it is written. Others insist, however, that the Bible cannot be interpreted that way and urge that the interpreter must have many technical skills to understand the Bible. Laymen have been confused by this conflict. They are still asking, "How can we rightly divide the Word of God?"

Making the Bible Relevant

Unfortunately, some people have fallen into such despair because of the controversy or their inability to find in the Bible precise answers to contemporary questions that they have decided that the Bible is not relevant to their situation.

Life is too precious to use it studying that which is irrelevant. Human resources are too valuable to squander on the acquisition of that which is irrelevant. There is no doubt that many interpretations and styles of the interpretations have made the Bible appear irrelevant. On the other hand, some extreme critics have made the Bible the victim of anemia. This book expresses the hope that the power of the Bible can be recovered to reveal its relevance and robust truth.

This goal will be attainable only when we follow the biblical injunction of "rightly dividing the word" (2 Tim. 2:15). The problem is not that the Bible is ignored. The refusal to take the Bible seriously is the result of either an anemic or irrelevant Bible. In turn an anemic or irrelevant Bible is the result of Christianity's failure in "rightly dividing the word."

The Loss of the Bible in Modern Religion

Undoubtedly there has been a loss of the Bible in modern religion. This has happened at the same time that Bibles have been selling at a record rate. It has happened despite the fact that the Bible has been translated into more languages than ever before. It has happened at a time the Bible has been translated into easy to read and highly understandable English.

The loss of the Bible in religion has not happened only in our time. Scriptures were physically lost at one point in Old Testament times. Read 2 Kings 22 for the story. The Temple had fallen into disrepair, and the new King Josiah wanted to return to the prophetic Hebrew religion. While men were refurbishing the Temple, they found a copy of the law which had been lost apparently for generations. The evidence indicates that what they found was the book of Deuteronomy.[1] It was a treasured find because every copy of the law had to be written by hand.

Today we produce millions of copies of the Bible each month through modern technology. Of course, the present generation has not lost the Bible physically. But it could be done whenever we might lose it spiritually. As long as Scriptures are seen to be instrumental in helping in daily living, and the preserver of the stories surrounding the events of divine revelation, the Bible will never be lost physically. It is much more difficult for the present generation to lose the Scriptures physically because of the mass production of the Bible today, but perhaps no less difficult to lose the

Scriptures spiritually.

The Scriptures become spiritually lost when they are replaced by tradition and official interpretations. They are spiritually lost to those who "go to seed" on a particular doctrine or idea. The perspective of the whole Bible must be kept or we lose God's Word spiritually. Whenever the Scriptures are neglected, they become spiritually lost. The same is true in anyway in which the Scriptures are misused. When the Bible is used as a fetish or a crystal ball, such misuse brings the spiritual loss of the Bible. The same is true with misinterpretations of the Bible whether through laziness or presumption.

Many copies of the Bible and all kinds of bindings may be available, but the Bible can still become spiritually lost. It is not unthinkable that the Bible might become physically lost if an atheistic government (such as is presently in power in Russia) should come to power in the Western world. There could be mass confiscation and destruction of Bibles. However, the greatest danger is that we will spiritually lose the Scriptures while inundated with a sea of Bibles of various translations and bindings.[2]

Recovering the Lost Bible

The recovery of the Scriptures is also a possibility. Again, the passage in 2 Kings 22 is an example of the spiritual recovery of the Bible. The dramatization of the king rending his clothes at the discovery of the lost Scriptures should dramatize our disturbance when we rediscover God's Word in the midst of all of the Bibles that are around. We will recover the Scriptures when we have a desperate need not unlike that of Judah in the seventh century B.C. It is not likely that we will spiritually rediscover all of the Scriptures at the same time but only a portion at a time.

Also, like Josiah, our discovery and recovery of the Bible will be dependent upon our acting upon the Scriptures. It will not be enough for us to read God's Word, but we will have to take it ultimately serious. I once read the story of a Scottish woman who heard her minister preach on Sunday. She sold fruit during the week and on her rounds she met the minister who had delivered the sermon. She complimented him on what a great sermon it was. The preacher, being accustomed to the "run of the mill" compliments on his sermons, teased the woman fruit peddler by asking, "If my sermon was so good, what did I preach about?" She answered, "I really don't remember, but afterward I went home and took the false bottom out of my fruit basket." The rediscovery of Scripture will happen when we act out the truth of Scripture.

The work of recovering the Scriptures is not an easy task. There is no easy way nor royal road to the understanding and application of the Bible. A person who wishes to open his Bible, put his finger on a verse, and suddenly have a revelation as to what that verse means is living in a demonic dreamland of silly superstition. Understanding and correct interpretation of Scripture only comes by the hard work of disciplined study, difficult decisions, sacrificial suffering, and human living. All these are a part of "rightly dividing the word" which goes far beyond the reading of pages in a book called the Bible.

Is a study about the Bible such as this one a relevant subject? It is. This belief comes from the conviction that the Bible preserves the very heart of God's revealing himself to man. Beyond this I will not try to prove with anxious arguments the validity of my conviction. However, I trust that each chapter in this book will be a window through which one can see the paths which have led me to this conviction.

2

The Book That Shapes Our Destiny

A major difference between man and the animal world is that the animal world is locked into a near meaningless cycle, but man has a destiny. Members of the animal world go through the cycle of birth, life, and death hardly aware of the history of their species. They write no history of their species and know nothing of the generations which preceded them except perhaps the mother which gave them birth. Neither does the animal world try to build a kingdom or idealize a future. They are locked into the perceptions of the days of their existence.

Man on the other hand does more than go through the cycle of birth, life, and death. His curiosity and ability has enabled him to write histories of his family and nation and even approach the writing of the history of his species, his earth, and his environment.

Man also is a kingdom builder. He tries to shape the future with trust funds, endowments, books, and other far-reaching legacies. He does not only plan for the next meal or the next evening's rest, but he seeks to plan the future ten years, a hundred years, and forever with his scientific, economic, philosophical, and political planning. Man is a kingdom builder who seeks to project and determine the society as it should be in the future as well as to influence the way society is at the present.

The most dramatic example of this tendency of man in the past century has been Marxism. The Marxists have tried to plan and promote what they believe will be the ideal society which man can achieve when the final state of communism appears. Even the distorted Marxist doctrine shows man exerting his humanity.

The Bible: Guide for Man's Pilgrimage

Man does not have complete control of the forces which influence his destiny, but he is the only creature on earth which has a destiny transcending the natural forces which work upon him. He is able to control those forces in such a way that they assist him in his achieving his destiny.

The Bible is the book which helps man shape that destiny. Apparently the animal world is left the victim of its instincts and the forces of nature. Man, however, transcends nature. He is not only a natural being but a historical being. Being a creature with a sense of destiny, there are ways in which man shapes that destiny. Men of Christian faith (and to some extent those who are not of Christian faith) have the Bible as a book to shape their destiny.

The destiny of man is like a pilgrimage. In the dim past the human race started out on a journey to find paradise lost. The pilgrim will find the slough of despair, the wicked city, and frivolous, faint-hearted and worldly companions on the way to his destination. While on the way, he needs all of the support, assistance, and companionship that true believers in the church of Jesus Christ can afford. The Bible, however, is the book that serves as a guide on this vital pilgrimage.

The Bible, as the book which shapes our destiny, spans the stretch of time beyond our own generation. This guide stretches beyond the accidents of history of one generation. This guidebook which shapes our destination transcends the changing cultures in which it was written, in which it has been interpreted, and in which we find ourselves now.

Other books have shaped various parts of man's world. Goethe's writings shaped the literature of the German language, and Shakespeare shaped the literature of the English-speaking world. Aristotle and Descartes wrote works which shaped the philosophy of the Western world. Bach, Beethoven, Mozart, and Handel have all shaped music of Western civilization. Copernicus shaped astronomy and Einstein shaped physics. Blackstone's writings shaped English jurisprudence and the American constitution has shaped the form of American government.

The Scriptures were not intended to shape music, philosophy, literature, or jurisprudence. The Bible was written for men whether they are musicians, philosophers, novelists, or lawyers. It is the book that shapes our destination, a destination which keeps moving like a huge powerful speeding missile into whose wake all human interests are being drawn. Other books may shape the destiny of a soldier, educator, or citizen, but the Bible shapes the destiny of man.

The Scriptures show us God's revelation as he shaped human destiny. Even those who participated in God's revelatory acts and those contemporary interpreters of those deeds did not always see with equal clarity the destiny which God had in mind for mankind. Not every passage in the Old Testament is as sublime as Isaiah 52 and 53, Job 38 to 41, or Psalm 90.

Every man of God who stood in that sacred tradition stood also in the midst of a particular culture into which the revelation of God came. There is no way to communicate the revelation of God without communicating the culture also, even though it is the revelation which is to be held as holy and not the culture into which it came. God's destiny for man pulsates throughout all of the cultures of mankind, but those cultures must not be mistaken for the destiny.

The Bible is the book which shapes our destiny, but it is not a guide for us to reduplicate a culture. It is a means through which we find the pulsating life of the revelation pointing to the destiny of man instead of following a side path of a cultural pattern which is only the garment in which revelation is clothed.

All other books are commentaries on Scripture whether they intend to be or not. It is the Bible that deals with man as a distinctive creature who has a destiny. Books on philosophy start with different presuppositions, but when they deal with ultimate reality or man's behavior, they have not escaped being commentaries on the message of the Bible—God's plan for the destiny of man. Authors may communicate stories of an individual's struggle, life, heroism, or deeds, but these are only isolated examples of human history as though an operator of a motion picture had stopped the machine to isolate only one frame.

The Bible itself is made up of many such isolated frames, but such isolated frames are only understood when the whole motion picture is seen. They serve as only sequential events in the whole story. When a master of literature makes an interpretation of the one frame, he is making a commentary upon this book (the Bible) which shapes our destiny. That commentary may be a poor one or a perceptive one.

Science books may not appear to be commentaries upon the Scriptures, but they may be among the most significant commentaries of our generation. The reductionism of science and the interpretation of all things in the scientific model may very well be a commentary on the Bible, denying the biblical position of the destiny of man and man's ultimate control over his destiny under the power of God.

The Inner Influence of the Bible

The Bible shapes our destiny, but it is not the only book which shapes our destiny. There are many books which have influence—strong influence—upon us. Karl Marx's *Das Kapital* has been a great influence upon each of our lives. Russian revolutionaries took Marx's ideas and made them into political and economic realities. Ever since then there has been economic competition, political spheres of influence and even military warfare. It is not that we wanted to be influenced by Marx, but we have been anyway.

When one reads the *Congressional Record,* he sees a book which contains speeches and laws which influence us greatly. These laws influence the makeup of our schools, income, and taxes and leave no area of our lives untouched.

These are books which shape our destiny from the outside. They are external influences upon our lives which have caused us to pay income taxes and send our friends and loved ones to foreign places because we felt the need to defend our kind of freedom.

When I speak of the Bible as being a book which shapes our destiny, I am not talking about its being that kind of an external influence. It is a book which shapes our destiny from within. We want the Bible to shape our destiny; therefore, we free it to shape our destiny from within. We are men of faith and because of our faith, we seek the guidance of the Book of faith.

No doubt there are men who are shaped by the Bible from without. It would be difficult for someone living in Western civilization to be untouched by the Judeo-Christian tradition, thought forms, and moral patterns. Even to reject these is to be shaped by them just as our rejection of Marxism shows that Marxism has influenced us.

During the Middle Ages, it was the goal of the Roman Church to make the influence of the Bible universal. That was an honorable goal that the church should always have. However, the problem in the Middle Ages was that the Church was content with making the Bible the book which shaped the destiny of people externally rather than from within. The result of the demand for external conformity was the Inquisition.

There is often the cry from Christian people to make the morality of the Scriptures the morality of the nation by means of congressional legislation. Such legislation and morality might very well be an improvement over the present legal system. However, that would be neither Christian nor scriptural morality. Christian and scriptural morality is not imposed from the outside but is the expression of faith response and obedience from within.

So the Bible is the book which shapes our destiny. Let us be careful to acknowledge that such is not automatically a reality. Even though we are Christian, the Bible does not automatically influence us as it should. We may buy a toy for our children for Christmas which must be assembled. We try and try to put it together but fail. The instructions are there, but we have never read them. They didn't fail us, we just didn't utilize them.

The Bible is like that as we try to assemble our lives and the course of human history. The Bible does not guide us in the assembling of life as it should be lived unless it is read. It is not enough, however, just to read the Bible. If one reads the instructions of how to assemble an article he has bought, he does not set them aside and ignore them but diligently tries to go through the instructions step by step. He carefully observes that what he has done is consistent with the pictures shown in the instructions. As important as it is to read the Bible worshipfully, devotionally, and scientifically, the Bible is only the guide to our destiny when we *live* it.

The Bible: Written for Man

The Bible is a resource book for man to fulfil his life and for mankind to fulfil its highest destiny. The Bible is a book written for man. Unfortunately, there are many who think of the Bible as a book which is written against man. They see the Bible as a law book to tell them what they cannot do and threaten them with judgments if they dare to do those forbidden things. Such an interpretation misses the whole purpose of the Bible. The Bible is not to keep man from doing something and going somewhere but to help man do what will make him the fullest man and help him to get to his highest destiny.

The highway needs signs which will help a person get to his destination. Some of those signs will mark the lane one should drive in if he is to execute the proper turn. They will mark what speed that turn can be taken in order to arrive safely where one wants to go. Signs are placed there in order to help a person get where he wants to go. Even stop signs and speed limit signs serve that purpose.

The Bible is filled with injunctions which in the long run will help us get where we want to go even though we may chafe under the admonitions. We may also be able to go over the speed limit or go through an intersection without stopping where there is a stop sign and not be arrested or have an accident. Sooner or later, however, such behavior will result in an occasion where we will never get where we want to go. We may find that the same principle holds true as we think about the Bible. We may get by from time to time disobeying the injunctions; however, in the long run such behavior will hinder us from getting where we want to go. It is in this way that the Bible was written for men, not against men. Thereby the Bible is the book that shapes our destiny as believing and practicing Christians.

The Bible shapes the destiny of individuals. It is persons as individuals who have faith and thereby seek the resources and guidance of the Bible. Individuals need not despair and think that the Bible was written for the great men of history. Leaders of a society need not despair feeling that the Bible was written only for the common man and the less complicated issues. The Bible deals with individual destiny. A part of our individual destiny is death and whatever is beyond it. The Bible clearly deals with this issue, culminating in the promise of Jesus' own resurrection as being the first-fruits of the destiny of those who are in Christ.

The Bible and the Human Family

The Bible does not deal only with the destiny of individual men but with the human race as a whole. Again, the analogy of the motion picture may be used: One may stop the projector on a single frame—the individual. However interested we may be in that individual, it is only when we see the whole film that we do justice to any individual frame. It is likely that if we are the one in an individual frame, we will want everyone to see that frame, the way we look, what we are doing, what is happening to us.

However important that frame is to us and those around us, "the show must go on." The whole film must be seen if that frame is to be fully appreciated. Concern does not end with the destiny of the individual. The Bible speaks of the destiny of the whole human race. God has plans not only for us individually but for all of his creation.

The Bible helps to shape the destiny of mankind because it shows what God has planned for that destiny. We are not mere automatons nor pawns on a chess board, but we are partners with God in his plan for the destiny of mankind. The Bible is like two pioneers plotting a chart where they will rendezvous in unexplored territory. We may not know the specific incidents of history between us and that point, but we know where we are headed. Some may cross rivers and mountains, and others may cross deserts and go through forests, but God has a destiny for his creation.

The Bible serves as a bench mark and the touchstone

for us as we lay out the territory of our lives. We constantly come back to the bench mark to find if we are laying out our lives within the proper boundaries which God has provided for us.

The Bible shapes our destiny by showing what is meaningful in the drama of our lives. The Bible is not just to be taken apart and looked at as several pieces, but we are to stand before the Bible for it to open depths of our spirits. People do not go to Niagara Falls in order to measure the chlorine content of the water or test the sediment. They go to the falls to see and hear the magnificence and splendor of them and to sense the drama which the falls arouse within them. It is true that one can measure the sediment and the chlorine content. Perhaps at times that is an important task. If one carried out those tasks, however, and missed having a sense of awe and wonder awakened by the falls, he would miss what the falls are uniquely capable of doing.

When we come to the Bible, we may very well be able to learn about ancient history, customs, and language, but we can do that and miss the powerfulness of the Bible. It is to awaken in us the dramatic meaningfulness of living life as a man in the image of God and to make us conscious of the destiny which God has for us. The Bible was not made for analysis but was made to awaken the spirits of men to turn toward God. Analysis is only valid when it can ultimately assist in that dramatic meaningfulness of awakening the spirit of man to the Spirit of God.

Sustenance for Spiritual Needs

The Bible has often supplied fresh energy to those who found it. Perhaps the greatest example of this was

THE BOOK THAT SHAPES OUR DESTINY

the Reformation where the Bible was rediscovered and applied to the Christian church and Christian living. What happened in the Reformation in such a dramatic way has happened since in individual lives and churches.

The Bible shapes our destiny by shaping our conscience. While each man is born with a conscience, that conscience is shaped by various forces. Many of us had the privilege of growing up in a Christian home where there was a reverence for the Bible and the encouragement to read and use the Bible. For those of us who came from such an upbringing it takes little introspection and self-honesty to recognize the Bible was a powerful force in shaping our conscience.

Men transcend the animal world and must have an environment which matches that special existence. The transcendence of man is his spiritual nature. That spiritual nature must have spiritual nourishment just as his physical nature must have physical nourishment. While our human spirits are nourished upon the Spirit of God, it is the Bible which directs us so that we are able to obtain that spiritual nourishment. In this way the Bible shapes our spiritual destiny. The Scriptures are important for our nourishment. While various traditions within historic Christianity have interpreted the Bible with different emphases, they have all recognized the need for the Bible in their Christian living and worship. James Smart observed,

Protestantism has long prided itself upon the attention that it gives to the Bible. Conservative churchmen have exalted it so unquestioningly that their attitude verges upon idolatry. Liberal churchmen have insisted that the question which the biblical text raises for a well-informed twentieth-century mind must be faced with honesty but rarely have they shown any information to remove the Bible from its central place in the worship of the Christian congregation or in the educational program of the church school.[1]

Once I attended a meeting at which were present clergymen from several of the historic Christian traditions. During the course of the days that we were together, I heard several conversations in which the clergymen criticized the theology of biblical writers. In worship periods, however, everyone of them expressed a deep and devout sense of devotion to the Scriptures and nourishment from them. Regardless of their words about the Bible, it was the book which had shaped their personal destiny.

Richard E. Palmer in his book, *Hermeneutics,* quoted Maurice Merleau-Ponty as saying: "Science manipulates things and gives up living in them" (p. 7). However important it is to approach the Scriptures in a scientific manner, sooner or later that is not enough. The real reason for approaching Scripture in the first place is not to do scientific analysis, but to be brought face to face with that dramatic moment of confrontation with God. Any scientific analysis has as its task to make that experience purer, clearer, and more vital.

3

God Speaks Through the Bible

The religious belief called deism professes that God is removed from the world which he created and does not communicate with it (or does so only seldomly). It claims that God doesn't speak to his world.

This was virtually the state of the Jewish religious leaders at the time when Jesus came. They had the law and the interpretations of the law so that they did not need any fresh revelation from God. They were quite self-sufficient with what they had. This is the reason John the Baptist and Jesus were such threats to the established religion. They did not attempt to give a new interpretation to the law but claimed to be the vehicles of God's revelation.

James Smart has written: "On the threshold of the New Testament we receive a warning of the peril to the revelation when the dialectic between the witness of the tradition and the continuing reality of revelation in the community of faith has dissolved. The movement forward is stopped. The faith of the community becomes frozen in its structures. The tradition is equated with the revelation so that there is no longer room in it for a John the Baptist or a Jesus." [1]

God's Invitation to Dialogue

When either a professed or a real deism grips us, we

are removed from the fruitfulness of God's action. Then we become observers of the world and the way God acted in the past. We need to be transformed into participants of the act of God's revelation in the here and now. Then we are no longer spectators only of the arena of the past where God acted in the lives of people, but we join the men of the past in the arena so that God's presence and revelation is real with us. We no longer just watch Jacob wrestling with the angel, but we become a participant in the confrontation with the heavenly hosts. We are no longer spectators who watch the characters speak to one another on the stage, but we mount the stage to take part in the dialogue.

It is like intermission time at the rock musical, *Godspell*. This intermission is unlike other intermissions where the actors and actresses retire to their dressing rooms. In *Godspell* the audience is invited up to the stage where they are served refreshments and converse with the actors and actresses. The Bible is like that. It invites us to participate in what it is trying to do. It invites us into dialogue with God.

The Bible becomes what it was meant to become only when God speaks through it. The real purpose of the Bible is not history, biography, sociology, philosophy, or doctrine; it is to be the instrument through which God speaks to every man who reads the Bible. Jesus Christ, who stood on the other side of the Scripture, whom we read about in the Bible, must confront us personally on this side of the Scripture. Just as Augustine heard the child say, "Take up and read," and found God speaking to him, we will find that God speaks through the Scriptures to us in our situation.

Now it must be clear that God speaks through the

Bible to our own situations. It is not enough that we read the words of Scripture or even memorize the words, but God must speak through the Scripture. In his book *Creative Ministry*, Henry Nouwen has put it well with one of the subtitles of a chapter, "Beyond the Transference of Knowledge." As important as the words of the Bible are, the main task of the Bible is not the transference of its words to our brains but as the sacred instrument through which God will speak his own message for us in our situation.

God speaks through the Scriptures. The Bible is not a dead book, but it is made alive again and again by the resounding voice of God. God's voice comes thundering down the judgment halls of the Bible. God's voice speaks forgiveness in the sanctuaries of the Bible. God's voice speaks tenderly in the homes of the Bible. It is ultimately important to hear the voice of God as He cries out through holy Scripture and confronts the God who speaks from the pages of the holy Scripture.

John Mackay wrote: "It is always possible to believe the Bible from cover to cover without uncovering the truth it contains. It is equally possible to know the historic truth regarding documents that make up the Bible and egregiously fail to hear the voice of the Eternal in biblical history." [2]

It is not the voice of biblical history, biblical interpretation, or biblical doctrine which is life-giving. It is the voice of God who speaks through the megaphone of the Bible. If we hear only the biblical history, interpretation, or doctrine, religious experience becomes second-hand experience rather than the vital saving experience of one's own confrontation with God.

James Smart spoke to that problem: "The Word of

God is not a set of truths and principles and rules, which, when once known, can be transmitted from man to man from that time on. Men have tried it again and again, and each time the words in which an age of great and vital faith expressed its truths and principles have become chains around the bodies and souls of the men of a succeeding age, robbing them of their freedom to hear for themselves and to find their way as men of a different age." [3]

This is the problem then—men read the Bible and listen to the Bible rather than listening for God. The Bible is a book of instruction, but it is also the instrument for the voice of God to speak to us in the here and now.

It was important for the church to define the books which would make up Christian Scripture. But it is a tragedy when people think that with the Bible God ceased to speak and that his voice can never be heard afresh. When this happens, someone takes over the function of speaking for God. It is only natural when this happens for official traditions and interpretations of Scripture to arise, such as happened in ancient Judaism, or for the church to empower someone to be the vicar of Christ on earth to speak authoritatively for Jesus Christ, such as happened in the Roman tradition. It is axiomatic that if God does not speak, someone will speak for him. "In many and various ways God spoke of old to our fathers by the prophets" (Heb. 1:1, RSV).

God has spoken to men in sundry ways. Karl Barth said that God's voice is not a monotonous voice but polyphonous. Barth meant that God spoke in many different ways with many different accents. [4]

Once when I was engaged in a study of the Chicano

movement in a Mexican-American community, I had
a young boy of about twelve as my guide to show me
what his world was like. During our conversation, he
spoke freely about his religion. He told his story about
a miracle that was supposed to have happened in Mex-
ico when Mary, the blessed virgin, had appeared. He
said she had told them that unless the world straight-
ened out it would be destroyed in a few years. I tried
to keep a smile off my face while devilishly I asked him
what language Mary spoke in to the Mexican people.
He answered without blinking "Spanish."

While I am not inclined to believe the boy's story
about the appearance of Mary, it does serve to illustrate
a truth about the revelation of God. Whenever God
speaks through the Bible, it is in the language of the
hearer. God speaks directly to men. It is not like a
recorded message on the telephone which is the same
if you dial once or twenty times.

God has spoken to everyone through the Bible who
has read it with faith, but certainly no one would say
that God has spoken to him out of every passage in the
Bible. God speaks to us out of our needs and our needs
have been such that certain passages have been the
clear bearer of God's voice to us, but other passages
have not been alive to our life situation.

God's Speaking and Our Preaching

God's speaking in this way holds some consequences
for preaching. It means that preaching through the
Bible book by book, chapter by chapter, and verse by
verse is an impossibility if preaching is to be in any
sense the minister echoing the voice of God which he
has heard in his own experience with Scripture and life.

He may, however, teach the Bible facts and interpretations verse by verse through the Bible.

The second implication for preaching is that preachers perhaps should rely more on dialogue preaching in
which the congregation shares with the preacher experiences in which they have heard the voice of God.
The minister may very well know the technical meaning of a passage and perhaps in a counseling situation
has seen the truth of a passage expressed in a person's
life. But only the person who is in the life situation
about which the passage speaks personally experiences
the voice of God in blessing or judgment. Such a person
may be able to preach the Word of God from a first-
hand experience with God because of his situation
which the minister could never do. This is one reason
why Fosdick could observe: "For one thing, spiritual
values are often discerned by a naive and childlike faith
when they are invisible to a critical and analytical
mind." [5]

Indeed passages of the Bible have remained silent for
long periods of time before unleashing their power
upon a situation. James Smart wrote: "The peculiar and
unique character of the scriptures is nowhere so apparent as in their ability to hide their meaning, sometimes
for long periods, from even the most intelligent and
earnest of men, and then suddenly to disclose their
meaning with revolutionary consequences in human
life. This is experienced both in the history of the
church and the history of individuals." [6]

God Speaks in Many Ways

Yes, God speaks through the Scriptures. A footnote
needs to be added, however, which says that God

speaks elsewhere, too. Myron Augsburger said: "The basic premise of biblical interpretation is to regard the Bible as a special revelation. As evangelical Christians we hold the Bible to be the Word of God written." [7] This is not to say that the pages of this book contain all that God has ever said to men.

No doubt God speaks from varying human situations in which we find ourselves. We have felt the presence of God very near in life situations. No doubt God speaks through world history. God speaks through our consciences. All of this does not detract from God speaking through the Bible because he has made it his special and sacred instrument through which he will speak his saving word over and over again. Even though God has chosen the Bible as such a sacred instrument through which he will speak, he is free. He will not allow us to box him in with only one instrument with which to speak, one weapon with which to fight, one language with which to speak or one voice with which to command.

The chapter began by talking about the deists who believe that God no longer communicated with his world. Perhaps the last step before deism is the limiting of God to speak only through the Bible.

4

Essential Elements in Rightly Dividing

When I first started to work on this chapter, I planned to call it, "The Bible as a Road Map." There are some reasons why the idea of a road map is a good analogy for the Bible. The Bible helps us achieve and arrive at the full, rich life we want in our earthly pilgrimage and the life with God on the other side of the curtain of death. As a road map helps one to get from where he is to a distant, unknown place, the Bible also helps us get to unknown places in living.

A map will have many points on it by which we can check to see if we are on the correct road and headed in the correct direction. We do not arrive immediately at our ultimate goal, but go through many intermediate points on the way. Likewise, the Bible will have many checkpoints for us to notice as we go through life to see if we are on the right road.

There is a difference between the road and the map. The reality is the road whereas the map is a guide along that road. There is also a difference between life and the Bible. The Bible gets us where we are meant to go in life.

You do not always need a map because you have passed over the terrain many times. I do not need a map to know how to get from my home to my office. When I go into a strange city, however, I may need a

map to go a much shorter distance. It may be that I
have lived certain aspects of my life until I know what
the roads are that I must follow to achieve the right
kind of life. Life, however, takes us into many strange
places where we have never been before. We constantly face new situations and in those situations, we
need a map. That map is the Bible.

When a person starts out with a road map, he must
examine it carefully to see where he is going, what
highway takes him there, and what are the checkpoints
along the way. Once he has these in mind, he keeps his
eyes on the road looking for the checkpoints. He recognizes them as a result of his study of the map. He may
stop occasionally and reevaluate where he is on his
journey to make sure he has plotted his course correctly. He does not, however, look at the map all of the
time. The Bible was not made for marathon reading but
to give us guidance in life. It is erroneous for a person
to travel through life without referring to the Bible as
his road map, but it is also erroneous for the monk in
a monastery to read the Bible aloud from early morning
all day into the night. The Bible was not made for mechanical reading but as a guide for life. We do not keep
our eyes on the road map (the Bible) all of the time, but
let the road map (the Bible) be our guide to where we
are going.

The Need for a Witness

The use of the analogy of the road map is a helpful
mechanism, but there is an element which is missing.
Unlike the road map, the Bible is not a cold document
setting out the precise measurements of longitude and
latitude. The Bible is more a witness to the trials found

in an uncharted area. The element that must be supplied is that the Bible is a witness. It is like a successful prospector writing to a friend about how he found gold.

For the man who follows the gold rush and wants to discover wealth for himself, he avidly seeks the meaning of every word. He tries to remember all of the procedures and the details. The instructions or books tell him about the kinds of places where he will likely find gold. They describe the kinds of rocks and caves where gold has been found. They describe the kinds of places in rivers where one might look for gold. They tell what to look for with descriptions of what their gold looks like. They go on to tell of the excitement of finding the gold.

Yet the would-be devotee of the gold rush does not have the book for his goal. The book is what helps to find gold. The book is the witness of one person who has found gold to another person who is seeking gold.

This analogy furnishes an important element missing in the previous analogy of the road map. That missing element is one man's joyful witness of good news to another man who is seeking the same experience.

The men of the Bible had experiences with God under many and varying circumstances. Their experiences were in differing cultures, under dissimilar stresses, primitive views of the world of science, with a different view of political states, with a less complex economic system. Yet they have testified how they met God in all of these circumstances. They left the Bible as a witness to the revelation of God which came in those varying circumstances. Whereas one man finds gold in the frozen Klondike, his witness of how he found gold inspires, guides, and helps another man in a more temperate region to make his own discovery of gold.

Men of varying backgrounds have given their witness which helps us in our own confrontation with God. John Havlik, associate director of evangelism for the Home Mission Board, Southern Baptist Convention, referred to the Bible as a witness. He observed: "The Bible not only witnesses to Christ but is itself a witness to the saving acts of God and the power of God in human lives." [1]

The exodus of Israel out of Egypt is a fact of ancient history. The Bible did not record the exodus experience to preserve facts of ancient history but to be the witness to the acts of God. They were confessing their faith that this was an act of God. This story was so much a confession of faith and a witness to an event of God's doing that it was turned into a creedal statement which was repeated many times in the Old Testament. (See Ps. 106:6–12.) A major festival season was created in order to commemorate it—the Passover.

The Bible is a witness of faith and not a neutral reporting using the scientific method of impartiality. The Bible does not give "just the facts" but gives the meaning of those facts. It witnesses to God's self-disclosure to man and man's response or rejection or faith. That witness can lead those who read the Bible to have a fresh encounter with God where he reveals himself through the experience of the reading of Scripture.

Recently, it has been popular to speak of the Bible as the record of revelation rather than the Bible being the revelation. For example, "The Baptist Faith and Message" of 1963 added: "The Holy Bible . . . is the record of God's revelation . . ." whereas that phrase was not in the 1925 "The Baptist Faith and Message" (See "The Baptist Faith and Message," p. 7). This addition no doubt emphasizes that God yet speaks in new and fresh encounters with men just as the Bible records those revelations which have become authoritative.

A further word needs to be added. A record filed in a courthouse may be seen as neutral, unbiased, unprejudiced evidence. The Bible is not that kind of record. It is a witness that something is true. It is not a neutral record but a *faith*ful witness. The Bible does not offer unbiased facts but the witness to the revelation because the witnesses believe in and are committed to the revelation. It is the same kind of difference as one might find between a geology report on geological formations of an area and a prospector's note on how he found gold in that area. The geologist might give a detached "scientific" report, but the prospector is personally involved in his witness to his findings.

Being Faithful to the Witness

So we have the book which witnesses to the reality of God and his self-revelation. It is a book that not only tells how others found that great treasure but it can lead us also to find our own treasure of experience with God. If we find that treasure, however, it will take something more than a book that tells us how. It will necessitate our understanding and correctly applying the truth of the book.

If someone gives a prospector directions on how he found gold, the prospector will follow it carefully in order to find his own "strike." If he fails to interpret the directions properly, he will likely fail as though he had no directions. If we are to find the riches of experiences with God, we must take the Bible seriously and follow it carefully. That is the task of "rightly dividing the word."

The task of "rightly dividing" is called hermeneutics. The word "hermeneutics" comes from a Greek word which points back to the Greek god Hermes—the wing-footed messenger. Richard E. Palmer says that the word "hermeneutics" means to express aloud in words, to explain, and to translate, and that all three may be expressed by the English verb "to interpret."

When the exhortation is given "rightly dividing," there is the implication that one may be guilty of "wrongly dividing." One author wrote a book entitled, *Rightly Dividing the Word of Truth,* and in the introduction he said: "The word of truth, then, has right divisions, and it must be evident that, as one cannot be 'a workman that needeth not to be ashamed' without observing them so any study of that word which ignores those Divisions must be in large measure profitless and confusing." [2]

But this author was so interested in giving *his* interpretation of Scripture that he was not careful in his interpretation. He assumed that the word of truth is *only* the Bible, but the Bible does not claim to have monopoly upon truth. He has taken the translation "rightly dividing" which has the verb "dividing" and translates that into a nonverbal form "right divisions." He has already decided that he is going to make seven different divisions out of the Bible so that his next step is to move from "right divisions" to Divisions (spelling it with a capital *D*). Whatever is the truth contained within his book, the text that he used for it is irrelevant to that truth.

This serves to illustrate one of the many dangers in biblical hermeneutics (or interpretation). When we have a point we want to prove, it often clouds our judgment as to the meaning of a specific text. We may even have a legitimate point but erroneously try to prove it by every passage of Scripture, by too many passages, or by the wrong passage.

This calls to mind the story of the preacher whose hobbyhorse was preaching on baptism. The deacons became weary of his one-subject sermons and finally asked him to preach a sermon on the first chapter of Genesis, which, of course, is far removed from the baptismal passages. The preacher agreed and on Sunday morning he began to go down the list of all the things that God had created; the earth, the sun, the moon, the trees. When he finally got to water he said, "and why did God make water if he didn't want us to baptize," and from thereon he continued his usual hobbyhorse of baptism.

Sometimes we are guilty of "wrongly dividing" by our sense of importance. There was a preacher I heard about who preached for three months on the flowers of the Bible. One wonders how even one such sermon could serve to bring a man in confrontation with God but three months' preaching on the flowers of the Bible indicates an unawareness of what is important within the Scriptures and the truth of God.

The Steps in "Rightly Dividing"

There are several steps in "rightly dividing." Some of these areas have already been touched upon and chapters which are to follow will deal with the others. The task ranges all of the way from taking a biblical text and finding out precisely what was written to the best of our ability to hearing God in the midst of our situation as he confronts us through the sacred text.

First of all, if one is to "rightly divide," he must find out what the author meant to say when he wrote a particular passage. Inasmuch as we cannot interview the author, we must rely upon the best manuscript of the Bible which we have available and all of the tools for working on that text. It may come as a surprise to some to find out that there are a variety of wordings of many passages in the Bible, Therefore, we have to use the tools of comparative texts, grammatical forms, historical materials, and literary composition in order to derive a basis for evaluating a particular passage. These same technical tools will have to be used over and over again to find out what the author originally had in mind. We will have to see how he used words, what were the historical events of his day, and how and why he put certain passages together.

Second, we will have to determine how a certain passage was "lived." The Bible did not appear out of a frozen, dead, and changeless situation but came out of a dynamic history that was taking place among God's people as well as changes taking place in the rest of the world. David's kingdom was not the same as that of the Roman Empire, nor was the theology of Jephthah the same as that of the apostle John.

Third, a text of Scripture cannot be understood except in the cultural context in which it was written. Each passage was written in a language of its day. The psychology, the thought forms, the institutions, and the symbols were all a part of each writer's own day.

Fourth, in order to know what a particular passage

means we must see how it fits into the picture of the whole of the Bible. Like a jigsaw puzzle, each passage is a part of the whole which contributes to the entire pattern. If we isolate a particular passage without taking the whole of the Bible into account, we are certain to miss the real significance of the passage.

Fifth, we must find the depth of what the Bible is dealing with. While a biblical passage may deal with this or that situation, it is also dealing with a deeper meaning. There is a spiritual depth to the issues which appear on the surface. Dealing with the events themselves is like a doctor dealing only with the symptoms and not the disease.

Sixth, in order to "rightly divide" we must deal with the relevance of the passage to our life situation. The Bible is relevant to our needs. If it were not, it would be a worthless book.

Seventh, "rightly dividing" means that the Bible must become an instrument for God's voice to speak to us. If our Bible study stops short of that, it has not gone the whole distance for which God gave us the Scriptures.

Rightly dividing the word of truth is no easy task. Some sincerely try to learn the biblical text and its background but fail to listen for the voice of God speaking in the here and now. There are others so anxious to achieve relevance and hear God's voice that they mistake their own voice echoing in a theological barrel or a demonic voice or the voice of the culture around them for God's voice. The following chapters will attempt to help us by serving as safeguards to keep those things from happening. However, there is no fail-safe in the process of "rightly dividing" the word of truth.

5

The Bible Is a Story

There is a great difference between a story and plain descriptive writing. Each of us has marvelled at watching a master teacher of children take some dull facts of history or science and weave them into a story and thereby keep children spellbound.

Jesus did this, too. Much of his preaching was done by parables. There is no doubt that this enhanced the memories of those who would write about Jesus later and helped them find ways to organize their materials. It was a way for Jesus to humanize the gospel instead of making it cold and austere. Such humanizing was consistent with the warm and compassionate personality of Jesus.

Also, there are things which can be communicated in a story which cannot be communicated in any other teaching method, especially when that material involves relationships between persons. A story carries with it, not only the spoken facts, but unspoken feelings. Whenever a story is told, the storyteller puts something of himself into it. He is not simply the narrator of the past. This is what Henry Nouwen, in his book *Creative Ministry,* was saying by the phrase "beyond retelling of the story."

The story carries with it a message which may or may not be capable of being directly told. Sometimes the message cannot be really told but must be "caught." There are times when to tell the point of the story in some other form of writing would destroy the whole context and interpersonal action which went on.

The Whole Bible Is One Story

When I talk about the story of the Bible, I am not talking about the story about the Bible, but that the Bible taken as a whole is a story which carries with it a message. Henry Chadwick pointed out that: "At first, of course, the word 'gospel' meant the message, not the book, and this is reflected in the second-century titles. It was the one Gospel of Jesus Christ, whether according to Mark, or Matthew, or Luke, or John. There were four versions of the story, four portraits of its central figure." [1]

Jesus Christ was the central point of the Bible story. It was his life that tied the whole of the Bible together and made sense out of all the diversities of laws, prophets, priests, poetry, dramas, histories, and the like. Sometimes in a play, a novel, or a movie there is one sentence uttered by a character around which the whole of the piece of literature revolves. If one misses that sentence, he is not able to grasp the significance of the whole play. Sometimes in a mystery novel there is one event or piece of evidence which is the clue of the whole mystery novel. Without that clue there is no reason for the existence of the novel at all. At times in a novel there is a central event which happens and all other events in the novel only set the stage for that central event. Scientific expositions and historical writings are not likely to have parallels to the centrality of an event of a story. The Bible is like the novel which

has a central point and a central event which is the clue
to the mystery of the Bible and the events or "word"
upon which the whole story of the Bible turns. That
central event and "word" is Jesus Christ.

The whole Bible makes up a story. Without the rest
of the Bible the life of Jesus would still be beautiful but
we would not really see the full significance of Jesus.
The story of the Bible begins in Genesis where God's
good creation is invaded by evil which separates God's
creature from God himself. The rest of the Bible is
related to the message of how God tries to bring about
a reconciliation between his creature, man, and himself. All of the other scenes in the Bible thicken the plot
which was set out in the first chapter of Genesis.

The separation which begins in the first chapter of
Genesis becomes wider and narrower at certain points
but never achieves the unity of God and man until the
full reconciliation which came at the central point of
the Bible in Jesus Christ who was man in whom dwelled
the fulness of the Godhead (see Col. 2:9). The remain-
der of the Bible is made up in showing how the message
of that reconciliation was bringing reconciliation to
reality in the world. The conclusion of the Bible is an
attempt to say that the future is in God's hands and he
will bring about final reconciliation in the end. The
Bible does not deal with just plain history but uses the
events of history to make a story which has a message
and in turn that story is a life-bearing and life-giving
message.

There was a man in a church where I was once a
pastor who was a master storyteller. He would begin
telling about an event but before long he would be
caught up in telling a side story because it was neces-

sary to know that side story to know what was important or funny about his main story. Sometimes one of
his stories would take an half an hour in telling because
he would have to tell enough side stories to make clear
the circumstances and the people involved in the cli-
mactic episode of the main story. The Bible also has
many side stories which are necessary if a person is to
grasp the central event—Jesus Christ.

There is no doubt but what some of these side stories
are much nearer the heart of the story itself than are
others. The church witnessed to this when it nearly
refused to accept such books as Esther and the Song of
Solomon into the canon of Scripture. Jesus was born out
of the womb of Hebrew faith and Jewish nationalism.
The intensity of those feelings can be understood more
clearly when one sees the intensive Jewishness of the
book of Esther even if the name of God is not within
it.

Perhaps the Song of Solomon helps us understand the
humanness of the people in the Hebrew tradition, and
the book of Ecclesiastes helps us see what happened to
a man when his Hebrew faith is subverted by Greek
philosophy. Certainly, if we had to choose between one
of these books and such books as Isaiah or Amos, we
would have to say that the latter books stand nearer the
central point (Jesus Christ) of the story of the Bible.
However, the richness of the Bible affords us these side
stories which help us understand the main movement
of the drama and the central point of the story.

The Unity and Pattern of the Bible

There is a unity to the Bible. But unity is not a unifor-
mity that makes a straight line; it is more like the lines

on a graph that show heights and depths. Because we know the norm of the chart, the heights and depths make sense to us. It is like the lines of a cardiogram. If there was only one straight line, it would mean either that the machine was out of order or that disaster had struck the patient. Because we know the pattern of the patient's heartbeats, we are able to make sense out of the varied vertical lines of the cardiogram. There is a unity about the cardiogram because it shows the different phases of the action of the heart.

There has been much discussion about the unity of the Bible, inasmuch as some have thought that each book and passage of the Bible had to say the same things and speak from the same viewpoints. That might have been so had the Bible been a scientific document written according to modern techniques. The Bible is a story made up of many side stories witnessing to the central event of the story—Jesus Christ. Each side story brings its own emphasis into the mainstream of the story of the Bible. Understanding the main story of the Bible depends on understanding the side stories of the Bible.

The pattern out of which the unity of the Bible comes is not obvious to all. It is not likely to be obvious to any except those of faith. In a test for color blindness there are hundreds of multicolored dots, but those who are color blind cannot see that some of these multicolored dots are so arranged to effect a numeral in the middle of those dots. One who has normal color vision immediately sees that there is a pattern of a numeral in the midst of the otherwise random placement of the colored dots.

The pattern in the story of the Bible is God trying

to bring man back together with him in reconciliation. It is not always obvious, however, until it is pointed out. We have all seen material in which there are patterns but missed what the pattern was until someone pointed it out to us. Then it was so obvious we wondered why we hadn't seen it before. Or we have played the game about seeing pictures in the clouds, and once someone has shown us that a particular cloud looks like a duck, immediately we can see it. Not everyone sees the story of the Bible and the pattern in the Bible. No doubt this is what led Jesus to say,"He that hath ears to hear, let him hear" (Matt. 11:15).

The reason both the Old and the New Testaments are needed is because they both are a part of the story. James Smart wrote: "A theology of the Old Testament would by its very nature be deficient, since it would leave out of consideration the most important and decisive events in the story of Israel in which the whole story comes to its climax, the advent of Jesus and the birth of the new Israel." [2]

While the New Testament by itself would have a character of beauty about it because of the personality of Jesus Christ and the drama of his followers, it needs the Old Testament to put in clear focus why the message of reconciliation in Jesus Christ was meaningful and necessary. If one had only the New Testament, it would be like coming into a play in the third act and seeing the denouement and finale. The hero and heroine might very well have their most dramatic parts and play them with their greatest skill during the third act, but one could not help but wonder what it was really all about.

My wife had a habit which annoyed me. She would

come into the TV room in the middle of a program. While I was trying to watch the progress of the drama, she would keep asking me: "Who is he?" "What did he do?" "What's happened so far?" "How did they get there?" While I was annoyed, I realized that she needed to know those things in order to unravel the thickening plot of the rest of the story. Proper knowledge of any section of Scripture depends on knowing the story of the Bible. Thereby the Bible is a unity. The New Testament by itself leaves us asking the question, how did we get here? The Old Testament by itself is incomplete without the final dramatic scene.

6

Living in Two Different Worlds

Much has been written about the generation gap. People who lived through or were raised during the depression years have different feelings and attitudes than do the young adults of today who are the products of an affluent society. There is also a huge generation gap between the biblical characters and ourselves. We live on the same earth as the biblical characters but not in the same world.

The difference between worlds can also be dramatized in the short history of our own country. The tracks made by covered wagons beginning their journeys of several months to California are still preserved at Fort Leavenworth, Kansas. Only ten miles away is a new modern airport with airplanes that carry 350 people to California in three hours instead of the six months it took the covered wagons. The Pony Express that left from nearby St. Joseph took several days to deliver a message to the West Coast, but now anyone of us can pick up a phone and in a matter of seconds get a message through to the West Coast.

We are geared up for our world, and it is an entirely different world than the one of Lewis and Clark. They mapped unexplored territory by taking keel boats up rivers, but we make exact charts from the photographs sent back from the satellites.

The World of Biblical Revelation

These changes which have been mentioned have happened in the last 150 years, but the Bible's personalities stretch out twenty times longer than that. If we cannot live in the world of our great-great grandfathers who lived in the frontier of our nation in the last century, certainly we cannot live in the same world as the Bible characters who lived twenty or thirty centuries ago in another part of the world, speaking another language and with different national traditions. Yes, we live on the same earth, but not in the same world.

Whenever we talk about revelation, we must also talk about the world into which it came. Revelation comes to particular men who have their own unique situations, who stand at a definite point in history, who speak a particular language and have their own understanding about how the universe operates. When the revelation comes to man, it demands a response from him. His response will be in the language that he knows rather than a language that is unknown to him or is not even yet in existence. He will respond with what he has.

The Hebrews responded in faith by offering sacrifices of animals to which they had access. They did not offer as sacrifices jet planes, television sets, or automobiles. The story of the revelation they received was written with quill on leather or parchment but not with the ballpoint pen, an electric typewriter, or stored electronically in a computer.

When the revelation came, it passed through the world of men. It is like the light which enters a great cathedral. That light passes through a beautiful stained-

glass window so that we have not only the natural sunlight but also the beauty of the colors in the glass. The
analogy goes beyond that because the sun passes
through the atmosphere where there are small particles off which the sun's rays reflect. We have often seen
that as we looked at a star and knew that its twinkle was
not due to the star itself but the atmosphere into which
the light comes.

A cook making gelatin is another illustration. She
puts the gelatin in a mold while the gelatin is still liquid.
After it has set, she puts it out onto a plate and the
gelatin has assumed the shape of the mold. Perhaps one
time she puts it in a round, smooth mold and another
time she puts it in a mold that is irregular or octagon
in shape. The gelatin assumes whatever shape the mold
is. It is the same gelatin whether it is put in a round,
irregular, or octagon mold. Another part of the analogy
is that the gelatin should be put in some kind of a mold
to set. There is no such thing as "shapeless" gelatin.

The revelation came to men in varying circumstances and cultural conditions. Just like the gelatin,
revelation had to come in some kind of a cultural and
historical context. It was the same revealing God who
revealed himself first in this historical circumstance and
then in some other cultural context. The point that the
apostle Paul made when he said, "We have this treasure
in earthen vessels" (2 Cor. 4:7) is applicable to this situation. We have the heavenly treasure of the gospel and
revelation in the earthen vessels of a specific historical
situation and a specific cultural context.

We live in a different historical situation and cultural
context. The revelation that came to Abraham was expressed in the cultural context of a pilgrim who grew

up in the Ur of Chaldees on his way to being a settler in Palestine. Had the revelation happened in the twentieth century, it would not have escaped a cultural context but would have been a different cultural context. He might have driven in a car instead of walking, or he might have brought company stocks and bonds instead of sheep. Either way the pilgrimage would have been a man's faithful response to God through the means available to him in his historical moment and in the possibilities available to him within his culture. Revelation not only has its divine side where God is opening himself up to man, but it has its human side where the expression of that revelation is made.

God has always sought to use man and the world in order to reveal himself. The great example of this is Jesus Christ who came as a man at a particular point in human history and in a particular culture. He was not a twentieth-century man but was God's revelation in the context of the first century in a mold that was prescientific, pretechnological and premodern. God did not seek to destroy the culture and history of that day but revealed himself through that culture and history.

H. H. Farmer has given an analogy picturing a hypothetical situation in which he is dropped from an airplane in the midst of a primitive tribe. He is to transform the people of that tribe into something far better than they have ever been. He has available any power that he wants to use to bring about these changes. Dr. Farmer sees that there are two possibilities open to him. He could use force to destroy the tribal organization and their primitive culture and replace it with his own plans and ideals. The second possibility would be that he could begin where the tribe is and find out what meaning their present life has for the tribe and lead them from that point to the worthwhile kind of life he wants them to have.[1]

It is obvious that the second way is the way God has chosen to bring about change in our world. He begins at the place where he encounters the human family and leads them to where he wants them to be. The incarnation illustrates this significant point. Jesus came as a Jew, a child of the first century, who lived his life trying to transform into a higher level the Jewishness out of which he had come. Jesus did not physically destroy Judaism but created out of Judaism a new people of God—the Christian church.

Once Jesus and the disciples, headed toward Jerusalem, stopped to spend the night in a Samaritan village. The Samaritans would not allow them to stay because of their identification with the Jewish people. The disciples wanted to call down fire and destroy the city but Jesus reprimanded them saying, "ye know not what manner of spirit ye are of" (Luke 9:55). This is an insight into God's attitude in revelation as expressed in its fullest in Jesus Christ. He did not come to destroy in order to reveal but to utilize what is present to express his revelation.

There are many things that served as the molds into which revelation came. Therefore, if we are to know the substance of revelation, we must be able to see what were the factors which shaped the expression of that revelation.

The Molds into Which Revelation Came

One of the important molds for understanding the

message of revelation is to understand the world view (cosmology) into which the revelation came. Many people expected Columbus to sail off the edge of the world because they thought that the world was flat. Columbus, however, journeyed to the New World and subsequently Magellan's crew, circumnavigating the earth, showed that the earth was round. We have also heard of the attacks against Copernicus, especially by the Roman Catholic Church, because he said that the earth circled around the sun rather than the sun moving around a stationary earth.

We have our own particular world view which is an unconscious factor shaping everything that we think. We are acquainted with the way airplanes use the curvature of the earth to fly the shortest distance from one point to another which is not a straight line across a flat map. We take for granted that astronauts went to the moon. One man I have heard about denies that men went to the moon saying that television has just made animated cartoons to deceive the public.

The revelation of God to which the Bible is a witness did not come to people with our world view. Perhaps most of the people during the period in which the Bible was written believed that the earth was flat. It was fourteen hundred years after the last book of the New Testament was written until Copernicus would announce his discovery that the earth revolved around the sun.

While there was a general world view in biblical days, there were many variations of that world view and the idea of the creation. Early civilizations had stories about creation and the world view. There were several of these by the time the Scriptures were written and a particular creation story and world view became the garment in which revelation was clothed. If we are to understand the substance of revelation in the creation story, we will have to understand the world view and creation story used in Scripture. We will also have to have knowledge about those creation stories and world views which were incompatible with the substance of revelation.

The psychology of a period is also important when studying factors which serve to express the subject of revelation. The idea of individualism is an example of one of the great differences between the Western civilization of the twentieth century and the period in which the Bible became the written witness of revelation. Western civilization is very individualistic. In fact in the United States the term "rugged individualism" has become a statement of the ideal way of life. Perhaps the latest expression of this individualism is the Women's Liberation movement. Advocates of this movement do not wish their identity to come from their husbands. Some have suggested that they should not take their husband's name upon marriage.

The psychology which prevailed among the people in the period in which the Bible was written was one of solidarity, mutual dependence and strong identification. There was a corporateness about the psychology in which a person did not think of himself as an individual but he thought of himself as an integral part of the group. He saw that the group expressed himself and that he in turn was an expression of the whole group and not just of his own self. This certainly was a factor which shaped the discussion of the effects of sin and redemption within the Bible. The earlier the Hebrew society the more intense was the display of social solidarity.

There was a sense of dependence which was present in the biblical tradition which was different from our stance today. People were much more vulnerable to the effects of nature. They did not understand the nature of natural catastrophe or disease, and they had almost no control over these. Therefore, the ancient people were much more conscious of their dependence upon nature than the present generation is. Therefore, the ancient expressions of feelings about nature is bound to be much different than those found in modern literature.

The people in the biblical tradition were part of a religious culture. The secularism of present-day Western civilization is a recent human development. Most civilizations which arose were religious cultures of some kind. This phenomenon lasted all the way through the Middle Ages. Inasmuch as they lived in a religious culture, they were bound to express their ideas in religious forms. Many periods of civilizations had such a strong sense of the sacred and so little sense of the secular that it was almost impossible to express an idea in secular terms (at least in purely secular terms).

The twentieth century is saturated with the idea of scientific method. Men of the twentieth century feel at home only with experimentation and observation. The saying "seeing is believing" really means "only seeing is believing." This kind of observation and experimentation is a recent development in history. The people in the Scriptures to whom the revelation came did not shape their expression of that experience with God according to the modern presuppositions of the scientific method.

The same can be said for technology. The shaping of hand-crafted tools, the simple potter's wheel, the beginning of the use of iron, and the introduction of chariots is hardly worthy of comparison to the technological complexity and sophistication of the twentieth century. The agricultural society of biblical times thought of the production of food, clothing, and shelter rather than the technological productivity which is foremost in the twentieth-century mind. An ancient writer could speak of his experience of revelation by saying, "Thou art my shepherd, I shall not want," but in his culture there was no way he could have said: "The Lord is my computer who has me programmed."

Past Revelation into Present Meaning

Now this is the crucial task for biblical interpretation that must be faced. How can one find the truth and the revelation in the Scriptures which was a revelation in another world even if upon the same earth. We are products of different ideas, feelings, pressures, information, and relationships than those who wrote expressing the revelatory act to them. Modern man, looking back at times when men did not have scientific understanding, feels as though they have really stepped into a "twilight zone."

There is an amusing story of a boy who was asked by his mother what he studied in Sunday School. The boy answered that they studied about the battle between the Egyptians and the Israelites when the Israelites crossed the Red Sea. His mother asked him to tell her what the Sunday School teacher had taught him. He told her that the Egyptian army came over the hill with their tanks and artillery so that the Israelites had to get into their pontoon boats and escape across the sea. He elaborated how the planes came down and tried to strafe them, but that the Israelites got away. His mother was shocked and said, "Surely your teacher didn't tell the story like that." The little boy answered, "No, but you would never believe it the way *she* told it."

I once read in a book written by Anne Morrow Lindberg about a worship service she attended deep within the Arctic Circle. She commented that the pastor substituted the phrase "the dynamite of God" for the phrase "the power of God." When she inquired about this, the pastor told her that the people there were not accustomed to the powerful forces of the industrial world but they were acquainted with the dynamite which was used to break up the ice in the harbors when the freezes trapped the ships in the Arctic harbor. They knew that the dynamite had to be powerful because of the huge geisers that they made and that also they could break up the ice when a huge ship could not break that ice. This is an example of an inventive minister trying to find a way to tell the story even if he had to go beyond the retelling of the story.[2]

There are many problems connected with trying to tell the story of the Bible today. One of the temptations is to stay with the form as it is in the Scriptures by using only the biblical words and images. Not only did the categories of expression have a sacred beginning but they have also been hallowed by twenty centuries of usage. Whenever we seek to use biblical categories we must remember the origin of these categories. The biblical forms, word, images, and categories were not in-

vented at the time of the writing of the Scriptures but
the human authors used the categories which were
available to them. The Scriptures were written in the
Hebrew, Aramaic, and Greek languages which were
common in their day and geographical region.[3]

Just as the Old Testament writers, the first-century
Christian used the finest and most adequate categories
that they possessed to express their witness to Jesus.
Even those lofty categories were categories already
available. They varied in their adequacy and inadequacy to express their witness to the sacred personality of Jesus. Even within the New Testament there
is the awareness of the inadequacy of certain categories
that the church used at first and the development of
new categories. One reason for this was the movement
of Christianity out of the Jewish community into the
Greek world. As the Christian faith moved from its
Jewish culture into a Greek culture, there were many
examples of utilizing images out of the non-Jewish
world to express Christian faith.

This is analagous to the situation we face in the twentieth century. We start with the images used in the Old
Testament and New Testament which represents
many slices of Semitic (Jewish) culture as well as the
culture of the Greco-Roman world. We attempt to tell
that same story with the same significance and same
meaning that the biblical writers told their generation
centuries ago.

The interpreter-translator faces serious dangers with
his task of attempting to make the Bible live in the
twentieth century. James Smart reminds us about this
when he says: "We unconsciously modernize the patriarchs, the prophets, Jesus and Paul, in our reading

of scripture, letting the elements fall away that are peculiar to their age and strange to ours." [4]

Smart said later: "For Renan he [Jesus] was one who would have been quite at home among the intellectuals of France in the mid-nineteenth century; for Bruce Barton he was a robust type of American idealist." [5]

The problem is that we may very well take our own images too seriously and not recognize the limitations that our own images have. Because of the great differences in cultures and the confusion of images, there is no way that one contemporary image can fulfil a biblical image. Edward Carpenter says it this way: "It has become almost commonplace to assert that the eighteenth century discovered in the gospels a rational Jesus; Schleiermacher, during the period of the romantic movement, a Jesus of feeling; the nineteenth century a liberal Jesus; and the twentieth against the background of war and revolution, a crisis or eschatological Jesus." [6]

In spite of all of these dangers, since the Bible is worthy of the adulation which it is given, we must attempt to show its relevance to the needs of men of our day. To do that we must put ourselves imaginatively into the life situations we find as we study the various passages of the Bible. The honest, sincere interpreter, who wants to make the Bible relevant to the needs of the people of his day for their salvation and sanctification, must live in two worlds—the world of the twentieth century and the world of the Bible.

Henry Chadwick, in discussing Origen, recognizes the criticism which has been made about the allegorical method. However, Chadwick points out that Origen's "final justification lies, perhaps, in the fact that by allegory he is able to make a scripture contemporary, more than a remote record of the distant past." [7]

The final purpose of the Bible is not for it to be encrusted in a kind of lacquer preservative but for it to serve as the unfailing guide needed in the world. The interpretation of the Bible in a relevant and meaningful way will probably always be a dangerous task which sometimes does not achieve perfect results such as happened with Origen. Nevertheless, because we believe that the Bible is God's special message and guide and because the Christian life is one that lives by faith anyway, the church will always undertake the task even with all of its risks.

7

Understanding the Dynamic of the Bible

The Bible is not a shallow, simple, and static book but a selection of writings whose dynamic comes from their witness to the purposeful revelation of God. The Bible is dynamic because its message is moving toward a goal as an arrow speeds for its target. From the first chapters it begins its goalward movement, but at times the direction may not always be clear, coming into better focus, however, as that goal is approached.

The fact that the Bible has this dynamic certainly sets it off from such religious literature as the sayings of Confucius. This is not to deny that those sayings are wise, literary gems, but they are only maxims and wise sayings. They do not tell a story nor head for a goal. There are maxims, proverbs, and wise sayings in the Bible, but these are particles caught up in the fast-flowing stream of the revelation.

Once a man was asked why he was reading the dictionary. He replied that it was pretty good reading except that there wasn't much plot. Religious books of maxims and proverbs may serve as practical dictionaries of everyday morals but lack dynamic thrust.

The Goal of the Biblical Revelation

It is very important to know the plot of the story and where the arrow of Scripture is headed. Without that the Bible cannot be correctly interpreted. Trying to do it is like making a long-range weather prediction by checking surface winds. They may be blowing at ground level from east to west, but several thousands of feet up the winds are blowing from west to east. One may be confused by surface eddies of air and forget the great prevailing winds. A part of the dynamic of the Bible is that its prevailing winds are headed toward goals even though in isolated instances one may detect the eddies around a particular historical situation which are blowing in another direction. Compare the tragedy of the Exile with the insight of Ezekiel.

Messianism (the idea of a coming Messiah) is one of the most obvious examples of the dynamic of the Bible. The sacred community, out of which the Bible came, understood that God had promised a messianic age in the future; this was God's goal in human history. The Chosen People did not attempt just to live their lives according to certain maxims and proverbs but to live their lives in the light of their hope for the messianic age. Sometimes they described the messianic age by talking about a messianic national community. At other times it was spoken of as a great battle with God's people as victors. Again, it was set in the context of a religious community and sometimes even personalized in a single individual. Nevertheless, they lived in the belief of the dynamic of what was going to happen and not just according to laws and proverbs. They believed that God would not cancel his covenant.

It is probably not an accident that during the time in which the Law was emphasized the most (such as in the time of Ezra) that messianism was emphasized the least and had to come to the forefront through unusual and dramatic means such as the apocalyptic literature found in portions of Joel, Zechariah, and Daniel. The witness of the Old Testament was not to a static set of laws or proverbs but to the use of laws and proverbs as building blocks for the great messianic act which God was going to fulfil in the future.

Many Directions but Still One Goal

There are many examples of the crosswinds and eddies which seemed to blow in opposite or different directions from the prevailing winds of the direction God wanted things to go. Yet many of these were necessary in order to shape history and the community out of which the messianic age would come.

Perhaps one of the greatest examples of this was the exile of Judah. At first it seemed as if God had forsaken his people; instead, it was an eddy going in the opposite direction from which God wanted things to go. The exile served as one of the greatest influences in the history of God's people to shape them as servants and instruments for the future purpose of God. For example, God's people were convinced that the Lord was their God but were nearsighted in not projecting him as the universal God of all mankind. They thought of him as a God of Palestine and especially of Jerusalem and most especially of the Temple in Jerusalem. As long as they were in Palestine and had the Temple, they would worship the Lord their God. But when Jerusalem was ravaged and the Temple was destroyed, their faith was challenged. Even worse, the people were taken captive into a foreign land. They could no longer think of their God as a Palestinian God or one who needed the Temple.

The exiled people of God either had to give up their God or had to expand their understanding of him into the God of the whole world who lived and worked outside of Palestine. The importance of this universalism is immeasurable in the life of God's people in preparation for the coming of Jesus Christ. He would not be just a Jewish savior but the Savior of the world. To be sure there was still objection to the universalism of Christianity. Even though it was resisted, the die had already been cast in the crosswind and the eddy of the exile more than five hundred years before the birth of our Lord.

It is possible to read the Bible in segments and never see the whole story and the movement of the dynamic of the Scriptures. It is like someone who looks at a painting with his eyes five inches from the canvas; he sees a glob of red paint here and a glob of brown paint there. Only when he moves back to view the whole canvas can he see that the painter has painted a beautiful sunset. Keep this in mind when examining the Bible word by word, verse by verse, and chapter by chapter. After studying the details, we must step back to see how they fit into the perspective of the whole canvas which God has painted.[1]

Understanding the Goal to Understand the Revelation

If the Bible is to be seen as a witness of the revelation of God, moving like an arrow toward its goal, it is necessary to judge the flight of the arrow according to where it is on its journey. This means that there are different stages in God's self-disclosure and the witness to that self-disclosure.

Myron Augsburger has observed: "Anabaptist Mennonite theology, from its very beginning, saw a distinction between the testaments. Not a distinction which questioned the 'grand unity' of the whole but one necessary if we are to see that unity. With this perspective a hermeneutic which sees the whole Bible as on a flat plane is unacceptable. It is evident in the Old Testament itself that it always has more to say about God. When one comes to the New Testament it is evident that the fullness of revelation is now provided in Christ." [2]

He went on to say something which may be a little over optimistic but yet provides help in biblical interpretation: "In scholarly scrutiny the so-called contradictions disappear when one sees levels of God's self-disclosure. The different levels in the unfolding of the divine will are steps to a higher level of perception. Matters which appear to be sub-Christian in the Old Testament are to be understood as levels in human experience which God had not as yet perfected the knowledge of his will." [3]

If a photograph were taken of an arrow in flight at any given point, it would not be the same as when it finally hits the bull's eye. Each passage of the Bible must be interpreted in light of its dynamic as though it were an arrow at a particular place headed toward its conclusion.

Another author dealt with the interpretative situation this way:

There are still problems that bother many readers of the Bible, particularly believing readers. What about things in the Bible which are really ungodly, any way you take them? There are, for example, some cursing Psalms. The author of

Psalm 137 rejoices to think of enemy babies having their heads bashed against a rock. The author of Psalm 69 also prays against his enemies; he asks God never to forgive them. Psalm 109 prays for the death of the Psalmist's enemy, prays that the enemy's children may be beggars, and that none may take pity on them. The Psalmist even prays that his enemy's father and mother may never have their sins forgiven. All this is far from Christian. If we are Christians we know we have no right to make such thoughts our own. Then how can it be revelation? The same can be said about Samuel's killing Agag, and condemning Saul for sparing the lives of babies and not committing total genocide—killing an entire race—today regarded as a serious crime.

For particular problems, these and others, the reader must consult the commentary. In general, we should be honest and confess that such things are not only pre-Christian, they are sub-Christian. We get into great moral confusion if we pretend otherwise. Such examples, however, may help us to realize that revelation is not sudden and complete; it is gradual. These ancient men of religion believed in the true God, but they had not yet fully understood his will. The revelation of God and his will, in the Bible, is like the growing light at sunrise; the first glimmers of the dawn are more dark than bright, yet it is genuine light. The dark is destined to dwindle, the dawn light will grow in Christ to the perfect day.[4]

The movements and change of ideas and institutions within the history of God's people is undeniable. It is false to apply only a mechanical evolutionary interpretive principle to explain this movement and change. God's revelation and his chosen witnesses are involved in that movement and change. However that revelation and witness happened in certain contexts (psychological, sociological, cultural, etc.).[5] This revelation and witness happened during certain historical crises, some of which were more intense and others less intense.

God's revelation meets varying levels of obedient response. Therefore there will be a great variety in the movement and change, but the Bible being a story means that it is headed toward certain conclusions.

Examples of the Dynamic of the Bible

There are some of these movements which can be plotted from their earlier level to their more complex level as though they were being placed upon a graph. There will be various high points which may be followed by somewhat lower points, but they will finally reach their peak.

One such movement is from the cultic emphasis to the ethical. The earliest experiences of the Old Testament emphasized the cultic far more than it did the ethical. This emphasis appeared in the necessity of certain rituals. Often the ethical law was identical with the performing of those rituals. The ethical emphasis became dominant by the end of the New Testament period. While worship and ritual were still practiced, the cultic acts were seen as fraudulent if they were not accompanied by ethical acts.

Another movement is from power to personal in the people's awareness of God. No better demonstration of this can be offered than to trace the emphasis on spirit in the early Old Testament and the height of the teaching about the Spirit in the New Testament. The early Old Testament passages speak of spirit in an impersonal way as a power which falls upon someone enabling him to perform unusual, cultic, or religious acts. There is no attempt to identify this spirit with the person of the Godhead. The New Testament certainly has some passages in which the Spirit is more power than personal, but the movement of the dynamic reaches its height when the Spirit is looked upon as highly personal, indeed, as the third member of the Trinity.[6]

Another movement within the Bible is from judgment to redemption. In spite of the great redemptive act for the nation as a result of its escaping the bondage of Egypt, the emphasis of the early Old Testament was upon future judgment for evildoers, even for those of the Hebrew tradition but especially for those outside that tradition. While judgment did not entirely disappear, in the New Testament the coming of Jesus Christ changed the emphasis to redemption. The pre-Christian messianism was filled with the idea of judgment upon the evil and the Gentile nations. However, the first Christians saw Jesus fulfilling the pre-Christian messianism but doing so by bringing redemption. The judgment of Christ was that he brought life while some preferred darkness rather than the light (see John 3: 16–21).

A movement parallel to that which went from judgment to redemption is the one which goes from retribution to love. Jesus himself pointed this out when he recalled the old ways of looking at things as "an eye for an eye and a tooth for a tooth" but admonished his disciples to turn the other cheek, to return good for evil, to go the second mile, to love those who despitefully used them, and to love their enemies. The peak of New Testament concern was reached when it was no longer trying to "get back" but trying to "bring back."

We often overlook the strong sense of tribalism which was felt by those of Old Testament times. So strong was that tribalism that it had not completely faded even in the New Testament where the genealogy of Jesus was related to a tribe and Paul could brag about being of the tribe of Benjamin. Tribalism was so strong in Old Testament times that it shaped the religious practices as well as the Hebrew customs and influenced the Scriptures. The stories of the Old Testament had to be experienced and/or preserved by someone who was a member of this or that tribe. The various tribes had their different versions of these stories and must have pushed to see that their version of the story was preserved. This is the reason why we have the repetition of stories, the stories told in two different ways, or the stories told more than once with different words being used.

Eventually, the twelve tribes were welded together into a united nation, but in reality that did not happen until Solomon. Tribalism was followed by an intense nationalism. Their God was Israel's God and they were jealous to keep him that way. Gradually the light of a new day of universalism began to break, although it was clouded over from time to time. Full universalism rose to its height in New Testament times when believers understood that Jesus Christ was not just a Jewish messiah but the Savior of the whole world. It was he who broke down the barriers between Jew and Gentile, male and female.

The dynamic movement within the Bible changed the focus from the earthly to the cosmic. The early Old Testament characters were busy digging a living out of the earth unaware of the cosmic dimensions of the universe. Whatever was significant for them was happening on earth. However, by the time of the New Testament, the outlook was cosmic and not just earthly.

Greatly influenced by apocalyptic literature (such as Daniel and Revelation), the people had widened the scope of their thinking about God's activity. They no longer saw God as just causing a pestilence to come to a community, but they saw him acting in the whole of creation.

Very close to that is the movement from the material to the spiritual. Early Hebrews thought that material goods were a sign of divine blessings. This had been developed to a fine art by the wealthy Jewish oligarchy. But the New Testament pictured valid blessings as spiritual rather than material. An example of this is in Luke's statement in the Sermon on the Mount: "Blessed are the poor," and Matthew's statement: "Blessed are the poor in spirit."

Perhaps one of the best illustrations of moving from material to the spiritual has to do with Jesus and the kingdom of God. Pre-Christian messianism was quite materialistic. It looked for the Messiah to set up a Jewish kingdom in Jerusalem from which he would expedite God's judgment upon the Gentile nations. Jesus spiritualized that concept of lordship and the kingdom of God. Whatever the kingdom of God may be at the end of time, the kingdom that the Messiah-Jesus described was a spiritual reign within the hearts of men.

The Scriptures formed a continuum from point A to point Z. God was involved at both points. It is not that Point Z does not negate point A; God had to deal with men within the cultural forms and thought forms in which he encountered them and at the level of obedience that he could expect from them. A man-made magnet in Manila cannot attract filings in Cleveland. It must be nearer to those steel filings in order to influence them. So it is that God does not deal with men at point *A* on the continuum from point *Z*, but he encounters men in the way in which he can influence them to move toward the point where he would have them to be. It is a part of interpreting Scripture to be able to see the continuum there is in it and to let Scripture stand in judgment as to where we are upon that continuum.

8

Just One Won't Work

No one method of study is final. Nor do all the aspects of any method apply equally to all areas of the Bible. The ore of scripture may be mined in different ways. The crucial test of a method is the end result, whether the method is able to get the gold from the ore.[1]

B. M. Metzger tells of the need of more than one method of interpretation. The Bible has too many facets for just one method. Just as every human is different, every penman has his own way of writing. The interpreter of Scripture will see that there were many different penmen, and he will be sensitive to that as he tries to interpret the writings. We must not come to the Bible with just one box into which we try to make everything fit. If our box is 3 by 5 feet, we should not force a seven-foot cane pole into it. What we need are appropriate boxes (methods of interpretation) to match the multi-shaped treasures within the Scriptures. If a passage is trying to communicate history, then an appropriate historical method should be used. But if the passage is ethical or apocalyptic, then other appropriate methods should be used.

Humility in Interpretation

This calls for real humility because we may not be completely prepared with all of the boxes (tools of interpretation) that we need for such a huge and multifaceted task. Our pride may very well get in our way because we have majored on only one kind of interpretation. We perhaps have found that one method of interpretation quite fruitful in getting results. Often we are unaware that we do use more than one method of interpretation even if we say that we use only one.

We also may have to admit from time to time that we do not have the right box available. That is a way of saying that we do not know the technical data that will allow us to make a correct interpretation. At times one method of interpretation does quite well and brings us to the heart of the subject even though another method of interpretation might have done all the first method did and have added a further dimension. Also as we find the key that unlocks one passage, it calls us to go back and reexamine a passage on which we have previously worked.

Simplicity and Interpretation

Simplicity has been a major goal of most Bible students. Science has awakened us to the fact that there is no real simplicity. A drop of water is not just a drop of water but an intricate dance of electrons, neutrons, and protons (and now they are finding realities beyond these). While everyone can use water without knowing all of these things, someone must know more about the complexities of water if we hope to use it for the suspension of medicine, intricate hydraulics, or as fuel cells.

If we approach the Bible simply, it can lead us to an initial commitment of our lives to Christ and salvation. But that is not the only level upon which the Bible was written nor is it the only level of human need. If we do

as Hebrews 6:1 says and "leave the elementary doctrines" to go to more complex problems with which the
Bible deals but then look back at that beginning commitment to Jesus Christ with disdain, we are guilty of
having used a tool to get where we are and then throw-
ing it away saying, "It is unusable." On the other hand,
the person who finds his beginning commitment to
Christ in a simple and nontechnical way will err if he
makes that the only method of approaching the Scriptures.

A surgeon or a dentist will use many different tools
to perform his intricate professional tasks, even though
to a "layman" they do not appear to be significantly
different tools. Just as we are "laymen" at surgery and
dentistry, we may also be laymen in biblical interpretation. However just as surgeons and dentists can make
mistakes and use the wrong tools or favor one tool over
another even though the other tool would be more
helpful, so the most competent biblical interpreters can
make mistakes of judgment or prejudice.

The Trap of Literalism

Where I went to preach once, the chairman of the
deacons invited me to share Sunday dinner with his
family. During the meal the deacon turned to me and
said, "I believe in taking every word of the Bible literally. Don't you?" Fortunately, at that moment someone
dropped the potatoes or something which so distracted
all of us that the question never had to be answered.
Later, I became interim pastor of the church and developed a strong friendship with the deacon and his
family. After an evening service one Sunday, I went to
the deacon's home. In his usual gracious way he com-

mented on my sermon of the evening. He said that he appreciated the new insight which the sermon had given him. He said he always wondered what the passage of Scripture meant because he knew the biblical writer never intended for us to take that passage literally.

I reminded my deacon friend of the conversation around the table some months previous. With his usual forthrightness and honesty, he said, "We always try to oversimplify things, don't we? And we shouldn't, especially with the Bible."

Of course there are passages in the Bible which are simply literal history. But that one method of interpretation is not the only one that is needed. Just one won't work! When Jesus held the unleavened bread at the Last Supper, he said, "This is my body" (Matt. 26:26). He obviously had something else in mind than identifying the unleavened bread literally with his body. When he took the cup of wine and said, "This is my blood," he did not mean that his veins had opened and flowed into the cup.

A literal interpretation is inadequate for the passage where Jesus said that a disciple must "hate his father and his mother." Nor do we literally follow the admonition of the Lord about praying that a mountain will be moved into the sea (Matt. 21:21–22). At least, all of the building committees that I have known in churches of various theological emphases have always used bulldozers in their building projects.

The reason that just one method of interpretation won't work is that we cannot be consistent when we use just one interpretation. For example, if we take the literal approach only, we find ways of deceiving ourselves into thinking that we are following that approach only while in fact we have devised some ingenious and subtle means of being nonliteral. For example, if I take a literal position toward the passage in Joshua (10:13) which says that the sun stood still, I am likely to try to find some way to make that passage square with modern science. According to modern science, it is the rotation of the earth that causes our days rather than the movement of the sun. Therefore, we might say that the earth stopped on its axis for a given period of time, or one might say that the earth dipped in its orbit so that a particular part of the planet was exposed to the sun longer. However, these explanations deal with the earth changing its usual pattern, but they do not say literally how the *sun* stood still.

Before Copernicus (1543) most people believed that the earth was a flat surface and the sun rose out of the ocean on one side and followed a circled track above the earth until it disappeared in the ocean on the other side at the end of the day. Whatever was the natural event which caused sunlight to last longer than usual, the world view in Joshua's time allowed them to say that the sun stopped that day just before it crashed into the sea. Of course, all of our modern explanations are based upon the Copernican view that the earth is round and circles the sun while rotating on its axis.

Harry Emerson Fosdick wrote about a man who was a real literalist. Fosdick reported:

Recently I received from a man in Massachusetts a letter contributing most human ills to the Copernican astronomy. Everything had gone wrong, he said, since men began believing in a round and moving earth. As for him, he was sure that alike Copernicus and Newton were wrong. The Scripture is against them, he wrote, and the facts sustained the Scriptures claim. He is the only thorough-going literalist with whom I ever dealt. He really believes the Bible from cover to cover. He has not deceived himself with any of those devious schemes by which less ingenious minds read into the first chapter of Genesis conceptions of the universe that never were thought of before the modern age.[2]

The next chapters will focus on some of the principles of interpretation. Each principle must be considered carefully as to its validity. However, the subject is more complex than that. It is not a matter of its validity in general, but whether it is a valid tool to use on a specific passage of Scripture. It may very well be that we should think of these tools of interpretation as keys. Perhaps one key opens most of the doors of the building. But some doors have two or more locks on the door and therefore they will take more than one key to get them open. Perhaps one key fits only one small door which is seldom used. That key would be inappropriate for all of the other doors, but it *is* necessary for that one door. Therefore, that particular key (principle of interpretation) could be inappropriate in the majority of situations.

As we go on, we should remember that whether it is literalism or an analytical method, just one won't work.

9

Here's How the Bible Does It

The writers of the New Testament used Scripture passages from the Old Testament in such a way as to indicate their special regard for them. They regarded those Scriptures as having sacredness about them. Usually scriptural quotations were introduced by such phrases as: "As it is written in Isaiah the prophet" (Mark 1:2, RSV); "You have heard that it was said" (Matt. 5:27, RSV); or "For so it is written by the prophet" (Matt. 2:5, RSV).

There were occasions when the biblical writers reflected on the nature of Scripture, such as the one time when the word inspiration is applied to Scripture in 2 Timothy 3:16, "All scripture is given by inspiration." Second Peter 1:21 also reflects upon the nature of the origin of Scripture when it says, "no prophecy ever came by the impulse of man, but men moved by the Holy Spirit spoken from God" (RSV).

There are very few reflective statements which consciously ponder the nature of the Scriptures. It is not from these passages, however, but from the New Testament's use of the Old Testament that we understand the quality of sacredness which the New Testament authors believed was a correct assessment of the Old Testament.

This is even more remarkable when we realize that

there had never been any final or official determination
about what would constitute sacred Scriptures of the
Jews at the time the New Testament was being written.
The writers of the New Testament also had to contend
with the Jewish commentaries called the *haggadah* and
halakah. While we now make a clear distinction between Scripture and these two kinds of commentaries
on Scripture, that separation between them has not
always been as clear as it is now.

The *halakah* provided detailed applications of Old
Testament laws, making them relevant to the circumstances of the later readers of the Old Testament. For
example, the *halakah* substituted financial compensa-
tion for the Old Testament demand of the literal
retaliation of "an eye for an eye and a tooth for a tooth."

The *haggadah* consisted of popular preaching where
biblical stories were retold but changed, added onto,
and embroidered to make some religious, ethical, or
political point out of the passages.

The Old Testament served in the New Testament to
clarify the understanding of Jesus as the Christ. New
Testament writers began with their own experience of
Jesus. He was the one who had dramatically changed
their lives and to whom they looked to come again with
the establishment of the kingdom of God. That was
their experience and belief in the face of several dis-
heartening situations: the fact that Jesus was no longer
with them physically, that the crucifixion was a scandal
to the Jews, and the incarnation was foolishness to the
Greeks. In order to bolster their belief that Jesus Christ
was really the Lord, they turned to the Old Testament.
There they found many stories, promises, words, and
coincidences which they used to clarify what they were

already saying about Jesus. They used these to defeat their opponents in debating the significance of Jesus.

While this could be understood to be effective and worthwhile in a Jewish culture, the New Testament has examples of this being used even in a Greek cultural context. The supreme example of this is the book of Hebrews. Its sophisticated use of the Greek language and its direction toward specific problems demonstrate that the book was meant for those who had more of a Greek cultural background than a Palestinian background, whether or not they were of Jewish racial heritage. The book of Hebrews applied Platonic philosophy as a means for expressing a great estimate of Jesus. This happened by welding together Greek philosophical forms with the materials from the Old Testament.

Beyond the New Testament view of Scripture lies the New Testament interpretation of it. The respect which the writers of the New Testament had for the Old Testament caused them to turn to these books. Because they looked at the Old Testament through the personality of Jesus Christ, they saw that there was gold to be mined in the Old Testament which the unbelieving Jews could not see.

The "Nonscientific" Method of Biblical Writers

Biblical scholars are accustomed to what is often called the "scientific" method of interpreting the Bible. While there might be many different emphases in "scientific" interpretation of Scripture, it does include the careful analysis of the text and alternate meanings, the background of the language, the context in which the passage was found, its literary form, the historical situation in which the passage was written including by whom and to whom it was written, and parallel passages and ideas.

The authors of the New Testament were nonscientific in their approach to the Scripture. This does not mean that they rejected the scientific approach any more than they rejected airplanes, cars, and television. The scientific method just had not been invented yet. Had the scientific method of interpretation been available to them and had they used it, there probably would have been several changes in the New Testament. First of all, the scientific method opens up some new avenues for seeing Christianity as the fulfilment of Old Testament religion. Secondly, they probably would not have used some of the arguments and passages which they did use in the same way they used them. Certainly the New Testament would have been much, much longer than it is now!

Recently a Bible professor, commenting upon a sermon of a doctoral student, complained that the sermon had been too brief; the chosen passage would deserve at least forty minutes for a proper exposition. In spite of the fact that the New Testament often used passages from the Old Testament, never once is there a real exposition of an Old Testament passage. Many New Testament passages refer to Old Testament passages, give interpretations of Old Testament passages, and relate Old Testament passages to such contemporary situations as the life and death of Jesus. However, the kind of emphasis on exposition which the Bible professor made and which all biblical scholars make today was not a part of the thinking of the writers of the New Testament.

This does not lessen our need for care and thoroughness in interpreting the Scriptures, but it does need to be recognized that we utilize an interpretive system which was not utilized in the New Testament.

New Testament interpretation of Scripture always made it relevant to the situation in which the New Testament writers found themselves. They related Old Testament times, such as messianism, the outpouring of the Spirit, and the influx of Gentiles into the faith.

Whatever method of interpretation was necessary in order to achieve that relevance, the writers would use it in order to bring about that relevant word. The allegorical method, alliteration, numerology, play on words, and other such devices were used by New Testament writers which might be avoided or shunned by many contemporary interpreters. The writers of the New Testament knew the gospel which they were going to present. They did not get that gospel out of the Scriptures but out of their experience with Jesus Christ. When they wrote the books of the New Testament, the writers used the Old Testament to describe, bolster, and illustrate their own experience with and conviction about Jesus Christ in order to convince others.[1]

The New Testament writers started with the conviction they had of Jesus and then began to find how the Old Testament affirmed this conviction. Their experience with Jesus Christ was primary and that experience determined their interest and interpretation of the Hebrew Scriptures. The modern interpreter may feel uncomfortable with that kind of approach.

Nevertheless, even if the New Testament writers did not have the scientific emphasis (which modern interpreters have), two things were uppermost in their minds. First, their experience with Jesus Christ left them with a conviction which shaped everything that they touched, including their reading of the Old Testament. Secondly, whatever else they did, they made the Old Testament relevant to the problems of New Testament times. They were not interested in just writing an exposition for intellectual curiosity but they were interested in applying Old Testament passages to the contemporary situation.

The New Testament writers believed that the Jewish Scriptures reflected real history. They did not accept the Old Testament as historical in the same way that modern scholars accept stories from the past as historical. The reason for this is that they did not have available the kinds of "scientific" historical methods that we have today, no more than they had available Copernicus' astronomy or Einstein's physics.

The Emphasis of the Biblical Writers

There was often an emphasis by the New Testament writers which was different from twentieth-century interpreters. Whenever they used the Old Testament, they used it as an example of what they were saying rather than an historical cause.[2]

The interest in literal history (which contemporary interpreters have) was not apparent in the New Testament. Today's emphasis is that if a passage is historical, keep it historical. If it is not historical, then understand it as nonhistorical so that the two are never confused. The New Testament writers, however, did not operate with those modern guidelines.

At times they took an event which was normally thought of as a historical event and made it relevant to a New Testament theme, even though there was no historical basis for the interpretation which they gave to it. The most obvious of such passages is 1 Corinthians 10 where Paul alludes to a rock from which the Hebrews drank during their pilgrimage with Moses. He talked about this being a spiritual rock which followed them even though there is nothing in the Old Testament Hebrew text which indicates anything but a stationary rock. Then he identified the rock with Christ.

This demonstrates two things. First, their ultimate seriousness about presenting Jesus Christ. Secondly, it illustrates that Paul was not so "uptight" about history as are most twentieth-century interpreters of Scripture. As necessary as the precautions are for our interpretation of Scripture, we must not foist those same cautions back onto the biblical writers.

Again, modern interpreters usually seek to avoid confessional interpretation as a principle of biblical interpretation. This kind of interpretation is involved when one takes a confession of faith, doctrine, or belief and makes a Scripture passage say the same thing as his confession of faith or doctrine. It is not difficult to see the reason for the reluctance of interpreters to use the confessional principle. There is no limit to the imagination as to how passages might be forced to speak falsely. As dangerous as it may seem to be, the New Testament often used the confessional principle of interpretation. The basic confession of the New Testament writers was "Jesus is Lord." Having experienced the lordship of Jesus Christ, they confessed that lordship. As a part of that confession, they collected many Old Testament references to interpret his birth, life, teachings, deeds, death, resurrection, and return.

The Bible's Use of Typology

Typology was another method of interpretation which was used by New Testament writers. It has never lost its appeal in the history of Christianity although it has been under severe criticism in the past few generations. The criticism has come from those who either demand a strictly literal interpretation or are consistent and thorough in their use of the historical-grammatical or the historical-critical approaches to biblical interpretation.

Typology says that something in the Old Testament is symbolic of a later event, person, or institution in the New Testament. A literalist cannot be consistent and use typology since literalists cannot accept the symbolic interpretation of scripture. Both the historical-grammatical and the historical-critical scholars are interested in finding out what the particular passage meant at the time at which it was written and under the circumstances of its writing. They would say that it is invalid and improper exposition to read into a passage something that was not there to begin with and specifically intended by the writer.[3]

In spite of modern reluctance to use typology, the New Testament made use of typology as a method of interpretation. One classical passage is Romans 5:14: "Yet death reigned from Adam to Moses, even over those whose sins were not like the transgression of Adam, who was a type of the one who was to come."

The Bible's Use of Allegory

Another method of interpretation which has fallen into disrepute is that of allegory. An allegory is the figurative treatment of one subject under the guise of another or a symbolic narrative. An allegory can be based on simple incident: a man rode his horse across a raging river filled with crocodiles to arrive safely in his loved one's arms on the other side. The allegorical interpreter might say: The rider is man on his life journey. The horse represents Christ and his faithfulness. The raging stream of crocodiles represents the evil world and the devil and his angels. The far shore represents the eternal, heavenly home. There is no doubt but what this is one of the most dangerous methods of interpretation. The literalists, historical-grammatical and historical-critical interpreters all agree on its dangers.

The allegorical method became a primary method of interpretation in the early post-apostolic church (see Chap. 10). The excesses of the early church led to the fear of its use later on. When scientific historical methods began to be applied to the Bible, the allegorical method was completely degraded. However, it was used in the New Testament. An example of the allegorical method is found in Galations where Paul himself said, "Now this is an allegory" (4:24, RSV).[4]

Typology and allegory, when used in the New Testament, were means and methods to express one's faith and experience with Jesus Christ. Those typologies and allegories were never taken so seriously as to be confused with that faith and experience in Jesus Christ. The question is whether an interpretation is to be creedal or to throw light on a subject. There were some creedal statements in the New Testament; however, most of the passages of the New Testament were not creedal but were to throw light on the experiences which they had had with Jesus Christ their Lord.

Interpretation in Christian Heritage

The New Testament took the history of the events of the Old Testament seriously. It affirmed that God had spoken through the events recorded in the Old Testament. Writers of the New Testament were also convinced that the Old Testament was the prelude to Jesus Christ. In fact it was their experience and faith in Jesus Christ which determined their interest and interpretation of the Old Testament. Some will object to this idea upon the grounds that the earliest disciples of Jesus were Jewish and would already have been interested in the Old Testament. My answer is that there is no indication in the New Testament that Peter, James, John, or any of the twelve had more than a usual acquaintance and interest in religious things including religious literature until Jesus said, "Follow me." The possible exception to this was that some might have been disciples of John the Baptist.

Therefore, these writers used a variety of methods of interpretation. Their concern was not the legitimacy of the method of interpretation but rather did the method of interpretation help them say what it was they had experienced with their Lord, Jesus Christ.

The Alexandrian Method

The controversy about interpretation began once

Christianity was cut loose from Judaism. The contention was no longer between Judaism and Christianity but between elements within Christianity. At the center of that contention was the allegorical method of interpretation.

The emphasis upon the allegorical method of interpretation arose from two sources. One of the sources was gnosticism. Some gnostics, such as Marcion, denied the Old Testament and also refused to accept certain books of the New Testament because of their Jewishness.

Others used the allegorical method of fanciful interpretation in order to avoid what they considered objectionable passages of the Old and New Testaments. This was consistent with their view of Christ which was docetic. Docetism believed that the material world and, therefore, the flesh were evil and not fully real. It was the spiritual which was real and worthy of the higher things. It is obvious by their logic that Jesus could not have been really physical but must have been only spiritual, and what the disciples and people of Jesus' day thought was his body was only a mirage or illusion.

The gnostics, therefore, could take the same dualism of the spiritual and physical and apply it to scriptural interpretation. The physical would be the literal explanation and the spiritual would be the hidden secret truth of Scripture known only by those who were true gnostics.

The second source of emphasis upon the allegorical method was Alexandria. The city was built by Alexander the Great and became a showpiece of transported Greek culture. A strong, Jewish colony settled in Alexandria and produced great Jewish scholars. It was from among these scholars that the Old Testament was first translated into Greek (the Septuagint).

A scholar by the name of Philo is the most remembered of the Alexandrian Jewish scholars. He had studied not only the Scriptures but also Greek philosophy. He tried to demonstrate that the wisdom of Judaism, when properly understood, did not differ from the greatest Greek philosophers.

Philo had seen how the Stoics used allegory by dividing truth into two classes—the physical and the ethical. The physical was any interpretation which referred to God or the world while the ethical was an interpretation which referred to the duties of man. Philo insisted that there were certain passages of the Old Testament where the literal interpretation must be denied because they contained something unworthy of God. Therefore, the alternative was to interpret that particular passage allegorically. Likewise, allegory was used when a passage seemed historically improbable or contained inconsistencies.

When Christianity was still young (mid-second century), a school of Christian scholars arose in Alexandria, too. It was only natural that they would emphasize the allegorical method because of the background of Jewish scholarship (Philo) in Alexandria. Egypt was also penetrated by the gnostics (Nag Hammadi). These Christians, therefore, had a double influence toward the use of the allegorical method.

Two of the great Christian scholars of Alexandria were Clement and Origen. These men differed from the gnostics inasmuch as they wanted to take Scripture seriously, even the Old Testament. This was one of the motives behind their use of the allegorical method.

Robert Grant summarized the Alexandrian Christian's approach this way: "Every word and syllable of scripture has its meaning but, since it was written symbolically, the meaning is usually not the obvious one." [1]

There was another reason for the Alexandrians to use the allegorical method. Just as Philo and the gnostics had found problems with a naive and literal interpretation of the Scriptures, the Alexandrian Christians also had to face this problem. Origen did not think that a historical interpretation of the Gospels was possible because of the discrepancies between the Gospels. He thought that if an interpreter held onto his faith in the Lord, he would either have to accept one of the four or admit that the truth is not in the letter of the writing but in symbolism contained in the Gospels.

Another reason for the use of allegory was that men like Origen thought that a literal interpretation of the Old Testament often led to a morally unworthy action on the part of God (such as commanding that uncircumcised children be killed). If something was unworthy of God when taken as historically true, then it must be symbolic of some truth. It was then that the allegorical method could be used to exploit that symbolism.

Robert Grant observed this about Augustine: "Only when he discovered the allegorical method of interpreting the Old Testament was he able to become a Christian." [2] This is why Grant also said: "the allegorical method, at a critical moment in Christian history, made it possible to uphold the rationality of the Christian faith." [3]

Origen was probably the first Christian who consciously worked out a theory of interpretation. He tried to parallel the interpretive principles to the Greek threefold view of man (which Origen also thought was consistent with the New Testament view of man). That three-fold view of man was the bodily, the psychic, and the spiritual. J. N. D. Kelly in his book *Early Christian Doctrines,* said that Origen's bodily view was concerned with "the straightforward historical events, and was useful for simple people." The psychic view involved "the moral sense, or the lesson of the text for the will." The spiritual view was "the mystic sense with relation to Christ, the church or the great truth of the faith." [4] Apparently, Origen connected the bodily interpretation with the historical interpretation, the psychic interpretation with the method of typology, and the spiritual interpretation with the allegorical method.

The Antiochene Method

The influence of the Alexandrian school arose to its greatest height in the last of the second century and the first half of the third century. Antioch as a sphere of influence in Christianity was a competitor in the last half of the third century and in the fourth century. Diodorus of Tarsus had two pupils who became bishops and spread the influence of the Antiochene exegesis.

The school at Antioch opposed the allegorical interpretation of Alexandria and developed its own interpretive method. E. C. Blackman has pointed out four characteristics the school at Antioch developed which stood in contradistinction to the school of Alexandria. He said: "First, the difference between the Old and the New Testament was more honestly recognized." [5] He pointed out in the second place that there was the "practice of studying a passage as a whole and in its context, and moreover in the context of the whole scripture, rather than in isolation, as a peg for some theory of his own or refutation of an opponent's theory." [6]

The third difference was that the "Antiochians not only rejected the subtleties and inner meanings of the Alexandrians, but also took up a more independent attitude to church tradition which the Alexandrians as well as their predecessors, Tertullian and Irenaeus, had upheld." [7] Lastly, Blackman observed that for the Antiochians "The inspiration of the scripture is no longer regarded as received in a trance or abnormal state—so the Alexandrians, claiming the authority of Plato—but as received through the quickening of the perception of the various biblical authors, through the heightening of their consciousness of spiritual matters rather than the suspension of consciousness." [8]

The basic difference between Antioch and Alexandria was that Antioch believed that allegory was an unreliable and illegitimate method of scriptural interpretation. Antioch developed *theoria* in place of the Alexandrian allegory. *Theoria* was the insight needed to understand certain Scriptures whose spiritual message extended beyond the explicit historical facts set out in the biblical text. *Theoria,* however, never did away with the historical basis and that was the radical departure from allegory. Thereby the Antiochians could use either of the interpretive methods—literal or *theoria.*

One of the greatest preachers of the early fathers was John Chrysostom, archbishop of Constantinople, who came out of the school of Antioch. His preaching consistently illustrated the Antiochian method. Theodore was the bishop of Mopsuestia (350–428). Theodore is usually regarded as the greatest interpreter of the school of Antioch.

The use of a more cautious type of exegesis was no assurance of orthodoxy. The second council of Constantinople (553) ordered the exegetical work of Theodore to be burned. They accused him of being responsible for the Christological errors of his pupil, Nestorius, and denying the inspiration of certain books which the church had agreed should be included in the Bible.

The school of Antioch with its literal-historical, exegetical method was strongly influential upon the thought of later Christianity. One special example of this was Jerome. His first commentary was pure allegory, but after he had come under the influence of the literal-historical method he forsook the allegorical method. Thereby, the Antioch literal-historical method was passed on to the later church.

Interpretation in Developing Christendom

Allegory did not die at the hands of the Antiochians. Augustine, bishop of Hippo, could not live without allegory in defending Christianity against its opponents. Also, allegory fitted well into his picture of the three types of inspired vision—corporal, spiritual and intellectual.

Controversies overshadowed the church's interest in scriptural interpretation. Much of the controversy arose around the politics of the Roman Empire and the politics of the church. The three great centers of religious-political power were Rome, Constantinople, and Alexandria. Issues were not always decided on the merits of the issue, but reasons were sought to disparage certain issues because of political alliances.

The great doctrinal controversies in the early church were over the nature and person of Christ. The statements of the early church dealt with the problem of Christ and the Trinity and did not deal with the nature of the Scriptures.

The early creeds of the church did not even mention the Scriptures. The Apostles' Creed, one of the oldest and most revered of the church creeds, contained no reference to Holy Scripture.[9]

Eusebius of Caesarea suggested that the Council of Nicaea (325) adopt the creed of his own church. They used it as a base to define orthodoxy in the creed they finally wrote. Neither the creed of Eusebius nor the Nicene Creed of 325 spoke of the Scriptures. Perhaps the first creed adopted by a church council which included a reference to the Scriptures was the one adopted by the Council at Chalcedon in 451. In it one statement referred to Scripture: "and arose again on the third day according to the scriptures." The church was not conscious of its dependence upon Scripture during those controversies. Many of the controversies were decided on the basis of philosophy rather than the Scriptures.

Many interpretive principles and interpretations were prevalent in the church of the early church fathers. Those leaders had to deal with the problem of literal or allegorical interpretation, but most of all they had to deal with heresies which threatened Christian faith or seemed to threaten it.

As mentioned before, there was no one method of interpretation that assured the purity and orthodoxy of Christian truth. Since there was no internal way to assure orthodoxy and purity, there had to be an external way to do so. First came the truth of Jesus Christ and secondly the entrusting of that to the apostles. However, both Jesus and the apostles were gone. That left the church standing in succession to Christ and his apostles as the guarantor of truth.

While interpreters on both sides of an issue of interpretation claimed the Scriptures to be on their side, someone had to decide which was correct. Both heresy and orthodoxy claimed the Scriptures, so another element had to brought in to settle the argument. That was tradition. This became solidified as the church began to decide what would be the official interpretation of the Scriptures and which would be official tradition. It did not make so much difference whether a literal or an allegorical method had been followed so long as it came out to be correct interpretation. Either method of interpretation might be followed, but what was important was that the church decided what particular interpretation was orthodox.

Since there was an official interpretation, the next step was to recognize an official interpreter. This finally came to be the pope in Roman Catholic tradition in the Vatican Council of 1870. Papal authority as absolute and ultimate, however, did not come automatically; it went through various states. The first stage was that of the council deciding what was orthodox and what was not. The next stage was to put this in a creedal form whereby further statements and theologians could be judged as to their orthodoxy. All of this implied that the church had the authority to decide what was the official interpretation and decide what was truth. This later led to recognizing the pope as the official interpreter of the church in Roman Catholic tradition.

This was an attempt to settle the problems of interpretations and orthodoxy. It did not settle the problems, however, but sowed the seeds for bringing about an unsettled condition. The unsettled condition arose because of lack of freedom which such official interpretation brought. Also, such official interpretations were vulnerable to further insight and evidence. The historical criticism of the Renaissance, the institutional challenge of the Reformation, and the spiritualism of the Anabaptists raised again the whole problem of church authority and official interpretation.

The Rise of Historical Science

Historical science arose in the Middle Ages. The substitution of historical presuppositions for doctrinal presuppositions was an unsettling event in the Roman Catholic Church. Lorenzo Valla used the developing methods of historical science to demonstrate that the document entitled "Donations of Constantine" was a forgery. Upon this document the Church had based its claim to its vast papal land holdings. After Valla the Church had no substantiation of those claims.

The principle of historical science (which Valla had used to show the false basis for the temporal power of the church) was turned upon other decrees of the church and, of course, upon the Scriptures themselves. By the time of the Middle Ages copies of the Bible had many marginal notes to clarify or to speculate about passages in the Scriptures. These were called glosses and were eventually copied into the texts parenthetically. Some glosses replaced parts of the textual material because the glosses more clearly demonstrated the official interpretation of the church. The original might not have been so clear or perhaps might even have been contradictory to the official interpretation. Historical science gave scholars the opportunity to clear away the improper glosses.

Philosophical presuppositions also arose as well as historical presuppositions. Some of the philosophical presuppositions were humanistic. Inasmuch as these interpreters were free from having to give the church's official interpretation, they offered a great variety of answers. Some of the interpreters either consciously or unconsciously opposed those official interpretations.

The rise of evolutionary presuppositions brought a new change in biblical interpretation. Evolutionary presuppositions wedded both historical inquiry and philosophical presuppositions into a new system. Just as the theory of evolution attempted to describe man as being a product of nature only, it also tried to explain man's religion in only naturalistic terms rather than in supernatural terms. Many interpreters faced serious difficulties because they realized the historical validity of many things that were being said by the evolutionists even though the evolutionists were basically and philosophically wrong.

Christianity became seriously divided at this point between those who would completely deny the new science and those who attempted to let the new science sharpen the tools of interpretation. The former often did not distinguish between the latter group and those who were unsympathetic to Christianity.

Scholars were still enamored with the use of historical science and tried to find through historical science what Jesus was really like. There were nearly as many different pictures of Jesus as there were interpreters. Albert Schweitzer at last put an end to the nineteenth-century quest for the historical Jesus by showing that every interpreter had claimed to be scientific but each came out with a different answer.[10]

Interpretation in the Twentieth Century

A young, Swiss pastor, Karl Barth, opened a new day for biblical interpretation when he opposed his church history professor, Adolf Harnack, by saying that one had to understand more than history for the Bible to be correctly interpreted. The interpreter must go beyond the grammatical and historical for him to interpret the Bible as the Word of God. He insisted that an interpreter must hear not only the words but what is behind the words. He must hear God's voice through the words.

Historical science has become a more refined and exact science in the twentieth century just as the natural sciences have. The result for biblical scholarship has been the development of literary criticism. Literary criticism is interested in the authorship of biblical books, the composition of the books, and the sources which lie behind the books. This study has been enhanced by the many new discoveries about the biblical text and information about groups and circumstances which existed during the time of the writing of the biblical material.

Form criticism followed the rise of literary criticism. Form criticism is interested in the significance of the structure or form of the biblical material. It is an attempt to find out how the forms in which the biblical writings have been put reflect the thought of the biblical writer is alien to the thought of the biblical writer.

Redaction criticism arose out of the former two kinds of investigation. Redaction criticism tries to find how the smaller units of biblical material were put together and why they were put together in the way they were. It believes that the faith of a church would influence the way the statements of Jesus which were preserved by the church were put together in the text.[11]

In summary it may be said that Christianity has gone through various stages of interpretation. Very early there were few rules of interpretation but much emphasis upon finding the meaning of Scripture necessary to sustain Christian faith. Inasmuch as this led to excesses, the church began to set some limits to principles of interpretation. This led to the grammatical-historical method of interpretation. There arose the need for orthodoxy to overshadow and protect correct biblical interpretation. By the Middle Ages a movement was under way back toward the historical-grammatical method, which would be a corrective to the church's demand for orthodoxy even at the sacrifice of adequate and accurate biblical interpretation. Further use of historical methodology brought the trend from grammatical-historical to grammatical-historical-critical biblical interpretation.

Now we face the failure of the technical approach to give complete sustenance to the Christian faith because the technical has become artificial in method and voluminous in words. The accompanying problem is the danger of the noncritical interpreter. The noncritical has allowed tradition—whether Catholic, Protestant, Anglican, or Evangelical—to be the determining factor in the interpretation of the Scriptures.

Interpretive Methods Illustrated

Many methods of interpretation have been alluded to during the course of this book. This chapter will show examples of some of these various methods of interpretation. Each example will risk clarity because it will be taken out of context. The whole passage would throw light on the method used and might help to show why the particular method was used. It is no doubt erroneous to think that any one method will meet every need (see chap. 7).

The Allegorical Method

The first type of interpretation which will be illustrated is the "allegorical." You will recall that this is an attempt to find a secret, hidden or "spiritual" meaning in a passage without being hampered by its literal sense or history.

The following illustration of the allegorical method was written by the powerful medieval abbot of the monastery at Clairvaux—Bernard. It relates to the story of Jacob's ladder found in Genesis 28:13.

This law, therefore, which leads to truth, St. Benedict arranges in twelve steps, in order that, just as we come to Christ after the ten commandments and the double circumcision (which make twelve), so we may apprehend truth by the ascent of these twelve steps. Moreover, what else is signified to us by the fact that the Lord was seen standing above the ladder which appeared to Jacob as a symbol of humility, but the fact that knowledge of truth is established at the summit of humility? For the Lord looked down from the top of the ladder upon the children of men, like Truth whose eyes neither deceive nor are deceived, to see if there were any that did understand, and seek God. Does he not seem to you to be crying from above and saying to those who seek him (for the Lord knoweth them that are his), *Come over to me, all ye that desire me, and be filled with my fruits;* and also, *Come unto me, all ye that labor and are heavy laden, and I will refresh you?* Come, he says. Whither? Unto me, Truth. How? Through humility. Why? I will refresh you. But what is the refreshment which Truth promises to those who are climbing and gives to those who reach the top? Is it love, perhaps? To this, as St. Benedict says, the monk will soon attain when he has mounted all the steps of humility. A truly sweet and pleasant food is love, which sustains the weary, strengthens the weak, rejoices the sad. It makes the yoke of Truth easy, and its burden light.[1]

The allegory has several parts. Bernard says that the ladder was the symbol of humility. He calls on the reader's imagination ("Does he not seem to you to be crying . . ."). He offers a sermonette that Truth promises refreshment to those who climb the ladder.

Regardless of the fine motives of the interpreter and the correctness of the point urged by the interpreter, in the allegorical method the fountain of the truth is elsewhere than the text.

Another example of allegory is found in Tertullian's writings. In writing about the parables in Luke 15, he said this about the lost coin (drachma).

Similarly, the parable of the drachma, as being called forth out of the same subject-matter, we equally interpret with reference to a heathen; albeit it had been "lost" in a house,

as it were in the church; albeit "found" by aid of a "lamp,"
as it were by aid of God's word. Nay, but this whole world
is the one house of all; in which world it is more the heathen,
who is found in darkness, whom the grace of God enlightens,
than the Christian, who is already in God's light. Finally, it
is *one* "straying" which is ascribed to the ewe and the
drachma: (and this is an evidence in my favour); for if the
parables had been composed with a view to a *Christian* sinner, after the loss of his faith, a *second* loss and restoration
of them would have been noted.[2]

Tertullian tried to sketch out each part of the story
to have its own meaning. Such complexity is character-
istic of allegory. Instead of there being one point to the
story (a parable), each part of the story is said to represent something other than the literal element.

This can be seen easily in Origen according to A. M.
Hunter's report of Origen's interpretation of the good
Samaritan:

The man who fell among thieves is Adam. As Jerusalem
represents heaven, so Jericho, to which the traveller journeyed, is the world. The robbers are man's enemies, the devil
and his minions. The priest stands for the Law, the Levite
for the prophets. The good Samaritan is Christ himself. The
beast on which the wounded man was set, is Christ's body
which bears the fallen Adam. The inn is the Church; the two
pence, the Father and the Son; and the Samaritan's promise
to come again, Christ's Second Advent.[3]

Such interpretation is colorful but not accurate.

The Devotional Approach

An approach to interpretation can seek the positive
teachings while ignoring the analytical aspects. Per-

haps this could be called the "devotional" approach. It does not attempt to deal with the "history" or the "elements" of a passage but exhorts from its words.

Matthew Henry lived prior to the great emphasis upon analytical examination of the Bible. Therefore, his writings are examples of the "devotional" type. Notice the example below.

His pulpit was a ship; not like Ezra's pulpit, that was *made for the purpose* (Neh. viii. 4); but converted to this use for want of a better. No place amiss for such a Preacher, whose presence dignified and consecrated any place; let not those who preach Christ be ashamed, though they have mean and inconvenient places to preach in. Some observe, that the people stood upon dry ground and firm ground, while the Preacher was upon the water in more hazard. Ministers are most exposed to trouble. Here was a true rostrum, a ship pulpit.[4]

Henry shows his method by his finding a "moral" in the fact that the people were on dry land but that the preacher was in the more hazardous position which indicates how ministers are most exposed to trouble.

The Literary-Historical Method

The literary-historical method was used by the authors of the volumes of the *International Critical Commentary*. Their purposes were: (1) to apply literary analysis to the literary style of a passage and (2) to evaluate the historical data of a passage in the light of general history, archaeology, and cultural backgrounds. This method is quite different from either the allegorical or devotional. It avoids sermonizing. An example appears on the next page: [5] You can see that the author's

XIV. 1-10. The people murmur at the report of the spies
(JE P).—To P belong at least v.² ⁵⁻⁷· ¹⁰ and part of v.¹, the
rest probably to JE ; see above, p. 132.

1 f. Disheartened by the report of the spies (13²⁷⁻³³) the
people lament and complain, and wish themselves already
dead in Egypt or the wilderness. As Di. has pointed out, the
subject is stated three times in these two verses; note the
three terms for the murmurers—*All the congregation* (1² phil.
n.), *the people, all the children of Israel* (cp. 20¹); the four
verbs—*they lifted up their voice* (ותשא ... ויתנו את קולם), *wept,
murmured*—might be progressive statements; but they are
more probably due in part to the fact that three sources are
here combined.—*And uttered their voice*] ויתנו את קולם Gn. 45²
(JE).—*And the people wept*] 11¹⁰· ¹³· ¹⁸· ²⁰ (J); cp. 25⁶ (P), 11⁴ (J).
—**2.** *That night*] CH. 142ᴶᴱ.—*And . . . murmured*] (וילנו) the
same verb (Niphal or Hiphil) in Ex. 15²⁴ 17³ (JE); otherwise,
like the noun (תלנות), it is confined to P or Rᴾ (CH. 114ʳ).—
Would that we had died in Egypt] cp. Ex. 14¹¹ᶠ· (J), 16³ (P), also
Nu. 20⁴ (P).—*In this wilderness*] v.²⁹.—**3, 4** (JE). The people
would rather return to Egypt than perish by the sword in the
attempt to conquer Canaan; they therefore propose to replace
Moses by another leader, who shall lead them back to Egypt.
It is not improbable that it was at this point in the narrative
of JE that Caleb came forward, stilled the people, and gave
an encouraging account of the land, 13³⁰.—*Why doth Yahweh
bring us into this land*] cp. v.⁸· ¹⁶· ²⁴.—*To fall by the sword*]
v.⁴³. The people fear the military power of the Canaanites
(13²⁸· ³²ᵇ· ³³); cp. Ex. 13¹⁷ (E). The complaint against Yahweh
is even more explicitly stated in Dt. 1²⁷. With the question
cp. Joshua's in Jos. 7⁷ (JE).

Between 13³³ and 14¹ S inserts, with the necessary change of persons,
Dt. 1²⁷⁻³³; see also Field's *Hexapla*; cp. the similar insertion before 13¹, and
see Introduction.—**1.** ויתנו . . . ותשא] The first verb agrees with the fem. subj.;

interest is only the reconstruction of the text and history.

The "Word Study" Approach

The "word study" method has been a popular type of interpretation in the past century; it combines some of the historical method with the devotional. It examines the many meanings which a particular word has had previously, and out of those meanings and contexts it finds a clarifying devotional significance. Sometimes even the tense of a verb is used to emphasize devotional meaning. Although the result sought is usually devotional, sometimes this method is also used to demonstrate a technical or doctrinal point. The following quotation illustrates the word study method:

(1:1) In the Greek text, the order of the words is, "At sundry times and in divers manners God spake." The Greek places his words at the beginning of a sentence for emphasis. Therefore, the main idea in the writer's mind here is not that God spake, but that it was at sundry times and in divers manners that He spake. He is not combating the denial of a revelation, but is preparing the reader for the truth that God has now, after the preliminary revelations, given a final word in the revelation of His Son.

The revelations of First Testament truth were given "at sundry times" *(polumeros)*. The word is made up of *polus* "many," and *meros* "parts," the total meaning being "by many portions." It was given also "in divers manners" *(polutropos)*. The word is made up of *polus* "many," and *tropos* "manner" or "fashion," thus, "different manners," or "many ways."

In the giving of the First Testament truth, God did not speak once for all, but in separate revelations, each of which set forth only a part of His will. One writer was given one, and another, another element of truth. God spoke in different ways. This does not refer to different ways in which He imparted His revelations to the writers, but to the difference of the various revelations in contents and form. He spoke to Israel in one way through Moses, in another, through Isaiah, etc. At the beginning of the revelation, the presentation was elementary. Later it appealed to a more developed spiritual sense. Again, the revelation differed according to the faithfulness or the unfaithfulness of Israel. Clement of Alexandria associates this passage with Ephesians 3:10, "the many-tinted *(polupoikilos)* wisdom of God."

The First Testament revelation was progressive. All could not be revealed at once, and because all could not be understood at once. Thus the revelation was given in many parts. In addition to this, it was given in different modes. It was given in the form of law, prophecy, history, psalm, sign, type, parable. *Expositor's* says that the people of Israel "were like men listening to a clock striking the hour, always getting nearer the truth but obliged to wait till the whole is heard."

The words "in times past" are the translation of *palai.* The Greek has two words meaning "old," *archaios,* meaning "old in point of time," and *palaios,* meaning "old in point of use, worn out, ready to be displaced by something new." The close association of our word *palai* to *palaios* suggests that the writer had in mind by its use, the fact that while the First Testament revelation was not to be cast aside, yet it was time for a new one to be given, one that would be God's final word, one that would complete and round out the first one.[6]

The Form Critical Method

Early in the twentieth century a new method of interpretation was created (or perfected). It has been more carefully defined than the types of interpretations which I have called the devotional or word study methods. The name which was given to this new method of interpretation was "form critical." The reason for the name is that it attempts to examine the literary forms which appear in the Scriptures. This method has been more thoroughly applied to the New Testament than to the Old Testament. Here is an example of "form critical" interpretation:

One more example out of a great number of similar cases may be mentioned: Luke 15:3–7 par. Matt. 18:12–14. According to Luke, the *parable of the Lost Sheep* was occasioned by the Pharisees' indignant protest that "this man receives sinners and eats with them" (15:2), and it closes (in Luke) with the words, "Even so, I tell you, there will be more joy in heaven (at the last judgment) over one sinner who repents than over ninety-nine righteous persons who need no repentance" (15:7). It was with the object of justifying the gospel against its critics that Jesus asserted, through a parable, that just as a shepherd, gathering his flock into the fold, rejoices over the lost sheep that he has found, so God rejoices over the repentant sinner. He rejoices because he can forgive. That, says Jesus, is why I receive sinners.

In Matthew the parable has an entirely different audience. According to 18:1 it is not addressed, as in Luke, to Jesus' opponents, but to his disciples; and accordingly the final sentence in Matthew has a different emphasis. It runs: "So it is not the will of my Father who is in heaven that one of these little ones should perish" (18:14). In the context of the admonition not to despise "one of these little ones" (v. 10), and of the instruction concerning the discipline of an erring brother (vv. 15–17), the concluding sentence clearly means: It is God's will that you should go after your backsliding brother —especially the "little," the weak, the helpless—as faithfully as the shepherd in the parable seeks the lost sheep. Thus, in Matthew the parable is addressed to the disciples, and calls on the leaders of the community to act as faithful shepherds towards those who fall away; the emphasis does not lie, as in Luke, on the shepherd's joy, but on the example of his persistent search. But the great instruction given in Matt. 18 to the leaders of the churches (for this is the chapter's intention, the usual interpretation of it as an instruction to the community being incorrect), in the context of which the Matthean parable stands, is a secondary composition, an expansion of the collection of sayings in Mark 9:33–50 (which are linked by catchword association). So the Matthean context does not help us to determine the original situation that led Jesus to tell the parable of the Lost Sheep. There can be no doubt that Luke has preserved the original situation. As in so many other instances, we have Jesus vindicating the good news against its critics, and declaring God's character, God's delight in forgiveness, as the reason why he himself received sinners.[7]

Obviously, there is no emphasis on the devotional meaning but an attempt to see the different forms a statement makes and attempting to see its original form.

The Method of Redaction Criticism

The most recent type of interpretation which has appeared is "redaction criticism." It attempts to see what the redactor (editor or writer) was trying to say by seeing how he put the various stories and sayings together and the themes connected with the passages that he used or omitted. A paragraph from the *Review and Expositor* of Southern Baptist Theological Seminary will illustrate this point.

C. The climax of our section is reached with the presentation of Jesus the Spirit-empowered preacher (4:14–30). The brief summary, Luke's own work (though guided by Mark), mentions not a word of the content of Jesus' preaching (4:14f); it sets the stage for the Nazareth encounter. Moreover, Luke does not want to present Jesus here as a preacher of the Kingdom of God, for he deleted this theme from the Markan summary which guided him in the writing of his own, and he by-passed it in the Nazareth sermon as well. Luke not only shifted the pericope from its Markan setting to its present prominent place but completely rewrote it as well. Scarcely a Markan phrase is left intact; the only real point of contact, apart from the general setting, are the question in v. 22 and the proverb in v. 24, both reformulated. Since both its present context and present content are congruent with Luke's outlook, it is reasonable to conclude that he is responsible for both. This means that here even more than in the baptism story Luke asserted his freedom to say what he wanted to say. This requires us to put special attention to this pericope if we are to grasp more precisely Luke's point.[8]

Professor Keck showed the unique concern of Luke by comparing the themes he used in a story as compared with the themes of another Gospel writer telling the same story. Thus, you not only hear the speaker's statement but also the writer's faith.

These methods of interpretation are the tools for the interpreter's task. They are not better (or worse) than the skill, discipline, and faith of the craftsman. Just as a car cannot be repaired with just one tool, the Bible does not yield to only one method of interpretation. We must be willing to utilize the proper tool for the proper function and not limit ourselves to only one because it is our favorite.

12

How to Know What a Passage Means

The meaning of the Bible is *not* always clear. The fact that there have been many varying interpretations through the centuries proves that. Had the Scriptures been self-evident in meaning, these would never have arisen. But our purpose here is not to discuss why God did not choose to give us a Bible which could not be misinterpreted but to find how we can be more proficient in the task of interpretation.

Tools for Interpretation

Ideally, interpretation would be easier if everyone had a knowledge of Hebrew, Aramaic, and Greek in order to examine the Scriptures in their original languages. Of course, that is unrealistic. Fortunately our generation has the unusual resources of a variety of versions of the Bible, both translations and paraphrases. Each one has some distinctive emphasis: the majesty of literature, technical accuracy of translation, or simplicity of style.

The interpreter should not limit himself to any one version of the Bible. The translators were human authors who approached their work with their own understanding and experience. One translator might very well have done a brilliant job with many of the passages assigned to him while another translator might have been able to draw richly from his own experience and give a translation of surpassing worth to other passages. Most translations of a particular passage will be complementary to one another. Therefore reading one version is like listening to a monaural record while reading more than one version is like listening to a stereo record. Additional versions can enrich understanding and interpretation.

Many books can be helpful to the interpreter. A concordance lists alphabetically every major word in the Bible and shows where they can be found. Commentaries give a verse-by-verse explanation of words and ideas. Bible atlases can help one understand the lands and people of the Bible.

Levels of Interpretation

We are accustomed to various levels of expertise, reality, and action in fields other than religion. A man may be a master mechanic of combustion engines but not have any kind of rating with a turbine or diesel engine. He may be able to do some work on them, but his expertise is in another field.

There are also various levels of biblical interpretation. The three levels which appear the most obvious are the historical, doctrinal, and experiential. An interpreter may work very well at the historical level but have no interest or skill at one of the other two levels. This means that a man may be able to understand archaeology, biblical language, the social customs of biblical times, and have intimate knowledge of the history of biblical times without having the interest or the ability to apply the Bible to contemporary moral situations. An interpreter may have a firm grasp on the literary mechanisms, such as literary, form, and redaction criticism but not be able to grasp the Bible as holy Scripture. An interpreter may have a grasp of the grammatical techniques of the Bible and the etymology of words without being able to hear the Word of God speaking through the Scriptures.

It would be difficult for someone to have a proper approach to the Bible doctrinally and experientially who did not have the proper understanding of it historically. Interpreting the Bible doctrinally is to try to find guidelines for belief which the Bible sets out for man. Interpreting the Bible experientially is to try to find the meaningfulness of the Bible for men individually and corporately.

Knowing What the Bible Means Historically

Knowing what the Bible means historically is the foundation stone upon which all other interpretation is set. This does not mean, however, that to know the Bible historically is a simple procedure which is easily come by. It is a difficult, perplexing, and exasperating discipline. It is a never-ending quest because we are constantly getting more information about the past as well as learning more about the text of the Scriptures.

If we are to understand the Bible historically, we must see how a passage fits into the whole scope of the Bible. The Bible is like a chart for land which people are traveling or exploring. If we are to understand a particular situation of a pilgrim, we will have to understand where he is on that pilgrimage. He may begin at a particular place because his chart calls for him to move from A to Z in some way other than in a straight line. Studying the chart as a whole helps us to understand how a particular passage marks a particular place on that chart.

The Bible is something like a patchwork quilt. When you look at the various patches individually before the sewing begins, they look as though they are random selections of cloth; but when they are sewn together a pattern emerges. The Bible is like that. We may not be able to see the pattern if we look at an isolated passage. Or even worse, we may think we understand the whole by looking at an isolated passage; its meaning may be quite different when related to the whole Bible.

This raises one of the crucial problems in understanding the Bible. We started out by saying that we must know the chart and where a particular passage fits on the chart before we can understand the Bible. This means that we must understand the Bible before we can understand the Bible. There is a sense in which that kind of circular reasoning is appropriate. We have to know something about what the Bible is about to begin with even though as we learn about individual passages of the Bible we may be able to make some minor adjustments to our chart. This dilemma points out the necessity of the church's teaching the Bible even though it should refrain from insisting on an official interpretation of every passage of the Bible.

Knowing what the Bible means historically also means that we must have a technical knowledge of the Bible. This technical knowledge of the Bible has most recently been called a "critical" knowledge of the Bible. The use of the word "critical" in any kind of historical science does not mean to be negative but means to examine carefully, to use technical tools of interpretation, to compare, and evaluate. The technical knowl-

edge we need of the Bible in order to know it historically includes knowing the various texts of the Bible,
the languages of the Bible, the culture of biblical times,
the geography of biblical lands, the dates and authors
of the biblical books, the historical conditions which
brought about their writing, the forms of literature
they represent, how they fit into the pattern of beliefs
of their times and their past, and how various authors
put together the materials which they had from the
revelatory events to form the books that they wrote.

The interpreter must also know the context of each
passage in order to know the Bible historically. A part
of that would be the literary context of a particular
passage. This means studying a passage in connection
with what goes before and what comes after it. It also
means to have an understanding of the historical context in which the passage was written.

An interpreter should have a kind of checklist to see
whether he is examining the passage thoroughly
enough. In that checklist it is obvious that a person
must understand the *historical events* which took place
about the time of the passage. He must also understand
the *literature* of the Bible as well as the surrounding
civilizations where the biblical literature was written.

The interpreter must know something about the *politics* of the period in which the passage was written and
the period which the passage portrays. An understanding of the *sociological factors* which were present at
the time of the writing and at the time that the writing
portrayed is necessary.

The *psychology* of the period in which the passage
is written is important in order to understand the decisions and reactions of the people. Often we are

tempted to think that everybody has always thought the way we think and had our kind of outlook.

The same thing is true about *science*. We must remember that everyone has not lived in our scientific age. People of Bible times had their own understanding about the principles of nature.

Also we must be aware of the *religious background* in which a passage was written. This means not only the religious institutions of the Judeo-Christian tradition but also the religions of those cultures which stood in opposition of the Judeo-Christian tradition. These influenced that tradition in one way or another.

If we are to know what the Bible means historically, we must relive the events of the Bible. It is impossible for us to modernize the ancient characters into our own day. They were the products of their day, their culture, their understanding, and their situation. It is necessary for us to relive the past if we are to understand them. James Smart warned about this when he said: "We unconsciously modernize the patriarchs, the prophets, Jesus and Paul in our reading of scripture, letting the elements fall away that are peculiar to their age and strange to ours." [1]

We must recreate as nearly as possible the whole picture of what the ancient days were like and walk with them in sandals on their dusty roads instead of inviting them to make transatlantic voyages with us on our supersonic jets. Only by doing that can we know what the Bible means historically.

Knowing What the Bible Means Doctrinally

Some Bible interpreters have attempted to talk about the Bible as being a book filled with doctrinal

axioms. These doctrinal axioms were looked upon as
eternally binding upon every generation. That is not
what is meant here by understanding the Bible doctrinally.

Understanding the Bible doctrinally means that
there are guidelines in belief which God has intended
for man and these are represented sufficiently in Holy
Scripture. While the former view of Bible doctrine
would lead to such conclusions as having to keep Satur-
day as the sabbath, animal sacrifice in the Temple, and
the Jewish dietary laws, this latter view of understanding the Bible doctrinally leads to no such conclusions.

How can we know the Bible doctrinally? First of all,
we must have some idea about what the author said and
what he thought he said. Thereby we can know what
it was that God was saying to him in the situation. It
is not always easy to find the principles and guides by
which God would have us live because they always had
to be given in the historical circumstances of a particular time. It is appropriate for us to take several of these
situations and see how God spoke through the cultural
situations to enunciate the doctrinal principle. This is
like someone using several points of reference such as
radio signals from several different stations in order to
locate exactly where he is. Checking the interrelations
of biblical experiences, precepts, and insights will lead
to the Bible's guidelines for faith.

Knowing What the Bible Means Experientially

One dimension in biblical interpretation goes
beyond historical and the formal commandments.
When we find ourselves in real life situations where we
face decision, disappointment, disillusionment, and

tragedy, we hear the voice of God through the Bible experientially in these situations. At these times all of our understanding of the Bible historically and doctrinally becomes only the bridge across which God comes to speak to us in our need.

In order for a passage to speak to us experientially, we must be committed to God and act upon the insight which he gives.

This is not some mechanical formula: If you do this, God will give you that, based upon some promise or generalization found in the Bible. To know the Bible experientially means that there is an intuitive inspiration which the Spirit of God gives to the committed listener.

Interpretation: Science or Art?

Interpretation of Scripture must answer this question. Are there definite principles which can be used in an objective way in order to arrive at a solution and interpretation which is correct? If it is to be a true science, it must be capable of utilizing these principles being used by anyone at any time and arrive at the same conclusions.

If the process of biblical interpretation is an art, then it comes by some kind of intuitive grasp or sensing of what God said or is trying to say in the Bible. An art is something which goes beyond science to grasp the intangible.

The answer is that the interpretation of Scripture is both a science and an art. At the level of the historical it is a science. What is history, literature, and grammar for one interpreter is the same for any interpreter. There are many ways in which doctrinal interpretation of the Bible is also a matter of science and not art. However, knowing the Bible experientially transcends the scientific method. When one begins to know the meaning of the Bible experientially, one becomes armed with the historical and doctrinal knowledge of the Bible which was gotten by science and not by art. However, understanding the Bible historically and doctrinally is only the runway from which one's experiential faith takes flight.

The Attitude of the Interpreter

If one is to be an interpreter of the Scriptures, he must be serious about it. One should not just dabble with medicine, radiation, or explosives. That can be very dangerous. A person should not play with psychiatry or hypnotism. In the same way a person should not dabble with the interpretation of Scripture but be very serious. He must be willing to pay the price of that seriousness.

An interpreter of the Bible should be reverent. He must realize that he stands on holy ground and before holy speech. This must not be interpreted as a way to take the Bible away from any examination and inspection. Just as a doctor examines a patient and treats him with respect because of the significance of humanity, so the interpreter approaches the Bible with reverence.

Honesty is a necessary attribute for the interpreter of Scripture. Every piece of evidence must be treated with forthrightness even if that evidence means that we have to revise some opinions.

The interpreter must be humble. The interpreter stands before God, and his life will be influenced and shaped by God speaking through the Scriptures. The proud and stubborn man will be deaf to God speaking to him through the Bible.

Patience is a proper attitude for the interpreter. Sometimes one must suspend judgment about a particular passage while waiting for evidence which will help to clarify it or for the insight which will show the meaning of the passage for one's own life. Most of us cannot expect to understand everything in the Bible. We must learn the meanings through the patient living out of the Scriptures day by day.

Interpreting the Bible is a study of faith. While the Bible may be looked at from a scientific and historical point of view by anyone who is intelligent and informed, the Bible cannot be known experientially except by faith. Until one stands committed to faith in God, he will not likely hear the voice of God in the Bible.

The interpretation of the Scriptures must be done in obedience. The fulness of the understanding of the Scriptures experientially can come only when a person shows his commitment of faith by obedience to the light which God gives him. Hearing the voice of God demands obedience to that voice in order for it to continue to speak.

It is not enough to be a reader of the Scriptures; one must be a hearer also. In order to be a real hearer of the voice of God in the Scriptures, one must also be a believer of the Word.

Notes

Chapter 1
[1] See the *Broadman Bible Commentary,* Vol. 3 (Nashville: Broadman Press, 1970), for a discussion of this.
[2] For a discussion of the loss of the Bible in modern religion see the book by James D. Smart, *The Strange Silence of the Bible in the Church* (Philadelphia: The Westminster Press, 1970).

Chapter 2
[1] James D. Smart, *ibid.,* p. 15.

Chapter 3
[1] *Ibid.,* p. 146.
[2] Quoted by E. C. Blackman in his book, *Biblical Interpretation* (London: London Independent Press Ltd., 1957), p. 13; he has quoted from John Mackay's book, *A Preface to Christian Theology* (New York: The Macmillan Co., 1941), p. 67.
[3] James D. Smart, *The Interpretation of Scripture* (Philadelphia: The Westminster Press, 1961), p. 53.
[4] Karl Barth, *Church Dogmatics* (Edinburg: T & T Clark, 1936), Vol. I, Sec. 1, pp. 111–123.
[5] Harry Emerson Fosdick, *The Modern Use of the Bible* (New York: The Macmillan Company, 1961), p. 174.
[6] James D. Smart, *The Interpretation of Scripture,* p. 13.
[7] Myron S. Augsburger, *Principles of Biblical Interpretation* (Scottdale, Pennsylvania: Herald Press, 1967), p. 8.

Chapter 4
[1] Wayne E. Ward and Joseph F. Green, *Is the Bible a Human Book?* (Nashville: Broadman Press, 1970), p. 113.
[2] C. I. Scofield, *Rightly Dividing the Word of Truth* (Bible Truth Depot, New York: Loizeaux Brothers, 1898), p. 2.

Chapter 5
[1] A quote by Henry Chadwick from the following book: Edward
Carpenter, *The Church's Use of the Bible,* edited by D. E. Nineham
(London: S.P.C.K., 1963), p. 31.
[2] James D. Smart, *The Interpretation of Scripture,* p. 21.

Chapter 6
[1] I want to thank John Claypool for calling this illustration to my
attention in the book, *Is the Bible a Human Book?* by Wayne E.
Ward and Joseph F. Green, p. 25.
[2] See Henri Nouwen's book, *Creative Ministry* (Garden City, New
York: Doubleday & Company, Inc., 1971).
[3] The Greek of the New Testament is known as koine Greek,
which meant "common" Greek, the Greek of the market and
home.
[4] James D. Smart, *The Interpretation of Scripture,* p. 37.
[5] *Ibid.*
[6] Edward Carpenter, *The Church's Use of the Bible,* p. 89.
[7] Henry Chadwick in Nineham's book, *The Church's Use of the
Bible,* p. 38.

Chapter 7
[1] One of the strengths of John Bright's book, *The Kingdom of God*
(New York: Abingdon Press, 1953), is that he sets the panorama of
how God has worked throughout the community of his people to
reach his goal.
[2] Myron S. Augsburger, *op. cit.,* p. 11.
[3] *Ibid.*
[4] B. M. Metzger, et al., *Introduction to the Bible, The Layman's
Bible Commentaries* (London: SCM Press Ltd., 1959), p. 23 f.
[5] See the previous chapter, "Living in Two Different Worlds."
[6] It is most interesting that this whole process of moving from
power to personal is seen in the Gospel of John.

Chapter 8
[1] B. M. Metzger, et al., *Ibid.,* p. 169.
[2] Harry Emerson Fosdick, *Ibid.,* p. 51 f.

Chapter 9
[1] This is a vital difference in principle of interpretation between
the writers of the New Testament and some contemporary scholars.
[2] There is a distinction which needs to be made between histori-

cal cause and typological cause. The latter is involved in the passages of the New Testament which were introduced by "in order that it might be fulfilled."

[3] Recently there has been a renewed interest in typology as is evident in the book, *Essays on Typology,* by G. W. H. Lampe, and K. J. Woollcombe (Naperville, Illinois: Alec R. Allenson, Inc., 1957).

[4] The Greek word used here is a participle root of the word allegory-allegoroumena.

Chapter 10

[1] Robert M. Grant, *A Short History of the Interpretation of the Bible* (New York: The Macmillan Company, 1948), 1963, p. 80.

[2] *Ibid.,* p. 109.

[3] *Ibid.,* p. 88.

[4] J. N. D. Kelly, *Early Christian Doctrines* (New York: Harper and Row).

[5] E. C. Blackman, *Biblical Interpretation* (London: Independent Press Ltd., 1957), p. 103.

[6] *Ibid.,* p. 104.

[7] *Ibid.,* p. 104.

[8] *Ibid.,* p. 105.

[9] Henry Bettenson, *Documents of the Christian Church* (New York & London: Oxford University Press, 1943, 1947), p. 34.

[10] See Albert Schweitzer, *The Quest of the Historical Jesus* (London: A. and C. Black, 1910).

[11] For a full statement of the subjects see Edgar V. McKnight, *What Is Form Criticism?* (Philadelphia: Fortress Press, 1969).

Chapter 11

[1] Bernard of Clairvaux, *The Steps of Humility,* translated by G. B. Burch (Notre Dame, Indiana: University of Notre Dame Press, 1963).

[2] The Rev. Alexander Roberts and James Donaldson, Editors, *The Ante-Nicene Fathers,* Vol. IV, p. 80.

[3] Archibald M. Hunter, *Interpreting the Parables* (Philadelphia: The Westminster Press, 1960), pp. 25–26.

[4] *Matthew Henry's Commentary* (New York: Fleming H. Revell Company, 1925), p. 180.

[5] George Buchanan Gray, *The International Critical Commentary, Numbers* (Edinburgh: T. & T. Clark, 1903), p. 152.

[6] Kenneth S. Wuest, *Hebrews in the Greek New Testament* (Grand Rapids: Wm. B. Eerdman's Publishing Co., 1953), pp. 31–32.

[7] Joachim, Jeremias, *Rediscovering the Parables* (New York: Charles Scribner's Sons, 1966), pp. 29–31.

[8] *Review & Expositor,* Gospel of Luke, Faculty of Southern Baptist Theological Seminary, Louisville, Kentucky, Fall, 1967, Vol. LXIV, No. 4, p. 477.

Chapter 12

[1] James D. Smart, *The Interpretation of Scripture,* p. 37.